A Century *and* Some Change

A
CENTURY
and
SOME CHANGE

MY LIFE
BEFORE THE *President*
CALLED MY NAME

Ann Nixon Cooper

WITH KAREN GRIGSBY BATES

ATRIA BOOKS

NEW YORK LONDON TORONTO SYDNEY

 **ATRIA** BOOKS

A Division of Simon & Schuster, Inc.
1230 Avenue of the Americas
New York, NY 10020

First Atria Books hardcover edition January 2010

ATRIA BOOKS and colophon are trademarks of Simon & Schuster, Inc.

For information about special discounts for bulk purchases,
please contact Simon & Schuster Special Sales at 1-866-506-1949
or business@simonandschuster.com.

The Simon & Schuster Speakers Bureau can bring authors to your live event.
For more information or to book an event, contact the Simon & Schuster Speakers
Bureau at 1-866-248-3049 or visit our website at www.simonspeakers.com.

Designed by Elliott Beard

The photographs on pages 143, 158, 159, 191, 194–195, 197, 200, 203, 204,
and 205 courtesy of Sally E. J. Warner. All other photographs are from the
author's collection.

Manufactured in the United States of America

10 9 8 7 6 5 4 3 2 1

Library of Congress Cataloging-in-Publication Data

Cooper, Ann Nixon, 1902–
A century and some change : my life before the president called my name /
Ann Nixon Cooper with Karen Grigsby Bates. — 1st Atria Books hardcover ed.
    p. cm.
1. Cooper, Ann Nixon, 1902– 2. Cooper, Ann Nixon, 1902– —Family.
3. African Americans—Biography. 4. African American women—Biography.
5. Centenarians—United States—Biography. 6. Shelbyville (Tenn.)—
Biography. 7. Nashville (Tenn.)—Biography. 8. Atlanta (Ga.)—Biography.
9. African Americans—Georgia—Atlanta—Social conditions—20th century.
10. Atlanta (Ga.)—Race relations—History—20th century. I. Bates, Karen
Grisby. II. Title.
E185.97.C76 A3 2010
973.9092—dc22

                                                                2009044552

ISBN 978-1-4391-5887-6
ISBN 978-1-4391-6393-1 (ebook)

In loving memory of my departed family:
My husband, Dr. A. B. Cooper Jr.,
Our children, Dr. Gwendolyn Mannings,
A. B. Cooper III, and Ann Marie Hooper.
And with special gratitude to Joyce Cooper Bobo,
whose love and support
continue to sustain me.
—Ann Nixon Cooper

To my family and families across America
who tell their history
and pass it on,
so the next generation
can do the same.
—Karen Grigsby Bates

CONTENTS

Contents

A Century *and* Some Change

CHAPTER ONE

Out and About

MY FAMILY STILL TEASES me that when the newly elected president of the United States called, I was on an outing with friends. Well, who knew? I go out all the time, even if I am over one hundred years old. I have many friends and social obligations, and I enjoy them all.

If someone had phoned ahead of time to tell me that Barack Obama was going to call, I would have stayed home. Probably. Sometimes, though, there are commitments you can't get out of; you don't want to disappoint people. But as it was, the call was a complete surprise.

My friend James Davis and I arrived back after a couple of hours out, and there was this lovely message on my machine from the presidential candidate—a long one, too! He said he had seen the story about me voting for him on CNN, and he wanted to thank me. That was nice. You could have knocked me over, I was so tickled.

As I said, I didn't think all that much of all the fuss about me going out to vote. Of course, my grandchildren and friends urged me to vote by mail, ahead of time. But I wasn't interested in that. Oh no! After all we'd been through as a people, if there was a black man who was a good candidate and he needed my vote, I was going to *be* there. I have been a registered voter since 1940, but this time—sixty-eight year later—I wanted to walk into that little booth and pull the curtain around me and vote. In person. For Barack Obama.

So that's exactly what I did. I put on my coral pink suit and my good-luck gold charm bracelet—the charms include numbers of my age from ninety-nine on up, and some lovely ones that mark my grandchildren's births. Atlanta mayor Shirley Franklin, who has been a friend for several years, came to meet me at the Fulton County Government Center, where the early voting was being held. She'd offered to meet me there to show her support that someone as old as me was determined to do her civic duty. I thought it was lovely of her to take the time to do that. There was also a handsome young newsman, an anchor person for CNN named Don Lemon, who guided my wheelchair into the polling site. (I like being escorted by handsome young men—always have.) I was surprised to see reporters and television crews from around Atlanta waiting with their cameras and recorders poised, all of them there just to watch me vote.

The voting process was "high tech," as my great grandchildren like to say. You just put your finger on a computer screen and touch the name of the candidate you want to elect. Casting my vote took only a minute, but it was an important one for me, my people, and my country.

After the story came out about Senator Obama calling and leaving me a message (I still have it), a few more reporters called and asked for an interview. I stayed quite busy for several weeks before election night.

On the evening of November 4, 2008, I watched with my family and friends as the nation elected its first black president. Around ten o'clock on election night the phone rang. It was someone from the president-elect's office. Mr. Obama had asked him to call me and let me know that Mr. Obama was going to use my name in his speech in an hour or so and ask if it was okay

with me. My answer was "Yes, of course!" I had the gentleman speak with Katrinka, my caregiver, and with my friend Sally, and we began passing the word around to as many friends and family we could reach on such short notice. And when President-elect Obama came onstage with his beautiful wife and their two pretty little girls to address all those people gathered in Grant Park, in Chicago, I was so proud. And then he made the speech:

> *This election had many firsts and many stories*
> *that will be told for generations. But one that's on*
> *my mind tonight is about a woman who cast her*
> *ballot in Atlanta. She's a lot like the millions of*
> *others who stood in line to make their voice heard*
> *in this election except for one thing. Ann Nixon*
> *Cooper is one hundred six years old.*

WELL, WE ALL WERE so tickled we opened a bottle of champagne to toast the new president. I think we were laughing and crying at the same time, because none

---

That's me and Atlanta mayor Shirley Hope Franklin at Shirley's office in November 2005. She's presenting me with this beautiful brooch and earrings.

---

of us thought this would happen in our lifetimes. So the fact that it *had* happened—that there seemed to be such joy in so much of the nation that we were starting fresh again—was a big part of our happiness. I went to bed a little while after and thought, Well, that's that. Now we're on our way.

Little did I know what the president-elect had started for me! My phone began to ring off the hook; it started while I was still in bed, continued all day and sometimes into the night, after I'd gone up to bed. The answering machine stayed so busy, I thought we might have to buy a new one! All of a sudden, everyone wanted to talk to me—Ann Louise Nixon Cooper. It was nice that they were interested, I guess. But I wasn't so thrilled that media and ordinary folk were acting as if the only exciting thing I'd ever done was vote for a black man for president.

Don't get me wrong, now. That was *plenty* exciting. But I'd had a life before CNN and the rest "discovered" me.

CHAPTER TWO

In the Beginning

A TLANTA, GEORGIA, HAS BEEN my home since September 1922. But I was born on January 9, 1902, in a little town called Shelbyville, in Bedford County, Tennessee, right outside of Nashville.

My father, James Henry Nixon, was a tenant farmer. That meant he worked on a piece of land that belonged to someone else, a white man. The arrangement was that Daddy got to keep half of what he produced, and the rest went to the farm owner. Daddy didn't make a lot of money, but he made enough to take care of our family. A lot of the provisions we needed were right at hand: we had chickens, a cow, and a big vegetable garden in our own backyard. And we traded with our neighbors for other things we needed.

Daddy worked long hours on the farm, but we always waited for him to come home before we had supper. My mother, Mollie George Nixon, would have everything ready by the time Daddy came home. He would greet us, go wash up, and then we'd sit down, he would say grace, and we'd have dinner together. Families don't eat meals together so much anymore, except on weekends or special occasions. This gave us a chance to keep up with each other, and I believe we were better off for doing so.

My mother took care of us children; she didn't work outside the home. There were eight of us all together, and I was third from the youngest. I had been the baby of the family for four whole years. And I loved being the youngest. All my sisters spoiled me something awful!

This is Langley Hall where my father worked and I played as a child. Langley Hall was built in 1903 by a single woman— Eleanor Katherine Trousdale—on land inherited from her uncle. Eleanor was called Katie and was the granddaughter of Governor William Trousdale. She later married William Young Allen, the president of the First People's Bank. ⟶∘❧

But I was happy when another sibling arrived, because then we had a boy, James Nixon Jr. And then the baby, Georgia Ruth. Finally, *I* could be a big sister!

My oldest sister was named Bessie Margaret, then came Mary Elizabeth, then Willie Lee. After her was Joyce Etta, and after Joyce came Grace Elizabeth. Then me. My name wasn't always Ann Louise. My mother had given all my sisters before me a middle name. She wanted the same for me, but after five girls, she was kind of stumped for an idea of what it could be. The midwife, an old white lady named Annie Lou Mullins, suggested Mama name me after her. Mama thought that was a good idea and named me Annie Lou Nixon.

I never much liked that name, so when I was old enough to get up the nerve, I asked Mama if I could change it.

"Well, what would you change it to?" she responded. She was so nice about it. She didn't laugh or tell me I

❦— *Here's my mother and her children in the field near our home in Shelbyville, Tennessee. We were bracketed by my mother on the left and my big sister Mary Elizabeth (her hands are in front of her) on the right. I'm leaning on the plow.*

was being silly, like a lot of adults would have. She just listened and decided that since I was going to be the one living with my name, I should maybe like it.

There was another white lady I knew named Miss Louise. I liked her and her name much more than I did Annie Lou Mullins, who was kind of coarse and sunburned. Miss Louise was pretty and rosy and refined. So I asked Mama could I shorten the first name and lengthen the middle one. So little Annie Lou Nixon became Ann Louise Nixon. Back then, where we lived, you didn't have to go to court and get a lawyer and go through all that you have to do now in some places to change your name. You just signed your new name on all your documents going forward, and after a while, that's who you were. Really, it was a luxury for our people to be *able* to change their names. For hundreds

---

I went with two of my older sisters and a family friend to sit for a portrait. Having your picture taken back then was an occasion—it wasn't point-and-shoot the way it is now. You made sure your hair was done, and your clothes were right, and you treated the photographer with respect. This group portrait shows (left to right) Joyce Nixon Harrison, me, our friend Rosetter Wade, and Mary Nixon Graves. Note our high-top shoes! —•⤜

of years before, we were given names by people who owned us, and we didn't have any say in the matter. So for a little colored girl to decide that her birth name was inadequate and change it (with her mother's permission), that was quite something.

My older sisters helped Mama around the house and in the vegetable garden. I did, too, when I got bigger. Before that, I would just follow them around and try to stay out of the way. My brother helped with yard work when he was old enough. He and I would feed the chickens, or pick the tomatoes, or sit on the porch with Mama and shell beans for dinner. Sometimes we got to run after one of the chickens and catch it and bring it to Mama. That would be our part of the job to get dinner on the table. Mama would wring its neck—quickly—and dunk it in hot water, then we would help pluck all the feathers out. And that night, we'd enjoy a nice chicken dinner. When Daddy killed a hog in the autumn, he and his brothers would cut it up and hang the meat in a smokehouse. Then we'd have ham and pork chops and pork roast to last all winter.

Besides keeping us fed and clean, our mother also taught us how to read, a skill that most of our neighbors did not have. Keep in mind that my grandparents were old enough to remember Emancipation from slavery, so it wasn't like black children were automatically educated when I was small. Colored children—that's what we called ourselves back then—mostly were expected to grow up and do work that required no formal education, certainly not work that required you to read.

My mother had grown up near a plantation. Her mother had worked for the white family that ran it, and she often took Mama to work with her. The white people there had taught Mama to read. I remember, when I was real little, people who lived near us would sometimes come to the door and ask Mama if she would read a letter they'd been sent. She would always put aside what she was doing and read for them.

Sometimes the letters were full of good news, announcing a wedding or a baby's birth, and Mama would be happy to read them aloud. Sometimes the news was sad, informing someone of an illness or a death, and she would have to speak gently to help them through it. Mama kept a little paper in the house because sometimes people wanted her to write a response. They were always so grateful and not only would thank her then but would often come back the next morning to leave a basket of eggs or a jar of preserves outside our door as a "thank you" to the Letter Lady.

Childish Things

WE LIVED IN THE country and were kind of isolated, so we were our own best company. After our chores were done, my sisters and I would play together and walk through the fields around our house as far as into the little woods at the edge of our property.

One day my sister Grace and I came home to hear a lot of laughter coming out of the house. What is this? we wondered. We walked in and saw our other sisters all around the kitchen table with their sleeves rolled up.

"What are y'all doing that's so funny?" we asked.

"We're marking ourselves!" And they sure had— they'd put their initials on the insides of their forearms.

"Why're you doing that?" we asked.

"So if we get lost in the woods, they'll know who we are!"

Well, it sounds crazy now, but it made sense to us at the time. You know how children think. Anyway, a little white girl had gone missing in the woods and her parents were frantic. I forget whether they ever found her or not. But my sisters' idea was that if the same terrible thing happened to us, we didn't want there to be any mistake in identifying us. So my older sisters decided to mark themselves up. Now, they didn't use an ink pen—it would be years before ballpoint pens were invented. Oh no—they were doing this with carbolic acid! When it's really diluted, carbolic acid is used as an antiseptic for wounds and infected bug bites and such. But straight out of the bottle, it was acid, plain and simple. Mama, who knew how to use it properly, kept it put away for safety's sake. My big sisters had found it and used it full-strength—a dangerous thing to do, since you could get poisoned. But they were fine, so I guess it's true about God protecting babes and fools.

Well, with that explanation, Grace and I insisted on being marked, too. So people would know who we were if *we* ever got lost. One of my older sisters offered to do it for us, but she warned us: "It's gonna burn." We wanted to do it anyway.

So they gave us a little twisted piece of cloth, and we dipped it into the acid, and we put our initials on our arms. Mine said A–L-N for Ann Louise Nixon, and it *did* hurt, but it looked kind of nice. The letters marked on our skin were raised and red, and we could tell, even then, that when the red went away, it would leave a fine scar.

We were all admiring our work and our toughness. We imagined that cows must feel like we did when they're seared with the branding iron. When Mama came home and saw what we'd done, she was horrified! Oh, did she make a fuss! She didn't spank us, though—maybe she felt we'd already done enough damage to ourselves—but she gave us a good talking-at, I tell you!

And then she made some balm and applied it to our arms, just clucking her tongue the whole time. But I think underneath, she had a little shadow of a smile. She knew she had some tough girls.

Lucky for us, none of us ever got lost in the woods, so nobody needed to look at our arms to figure out we were the Nixon girls. Those scars lasted for years before they finally faded away. I guess this was the early version of tattoos, something crazy that kids do to themselves today.

CHAPTER THREE

In the Valley of the Shadow

MY FATHER'S BROTHERS HAD moved away from the country to Nashville, the state's capital city. That's where the jobs were, they said. So they wanted us to join them there. But my father wasn't so interested. He liked having us all close together out there in Bedford County.

He and Mama had gotten married when they were real young—so young that one of my father's brothers had to sign his permission for them to marry. I don't know how Mama's family felt about that; we never really met any of them. I wonder to this day if the reason we didn't see them was because they were upset that she had married Daddy when she was so young. None of them came to her wedding, so we can only guess. Daddy and Mama were enough for us, though, and we didn't miss having grandparents. Our lives were busy and full.

But things changed drastically a few days after my eleventh birthday. Mama kissed us, left the house, and we never saw her alive again. She was going to visit the neighbors to thank them for our Christmas presents and collapsed while she was visiting.

From what I recall, she just . . . died. I'll never forget the date: January 13. The cause of her death could have been a heart attack or a stroke, but we'll never know. This was before the days of ultrasounds and MRIs and all those tests they give you to determine what is wrong when you're struck down like that. All I know is that Daddy came in to see us and sat us children down and told us the terrible news. It didn't make sense to us—we had just seen her that morning, leaving in a pretty new dress she had made to go around on her thank-you visits. Daddy was crying so hard he could hardly speak. I can't tell you which I found more shocking—that Mama was dead or that Daddy was crying. We had never seen him cry, ever. We knew our world as we'd known it was ending.

Friends carried Mama back, but they wouldn't let us see her up close. They put all us kids in the kitchen while they placed her in the front room. Some women came and washed her body and laid it out so we could say good-bye. She still looked like pretty Mama to us. And the next day they buried her. Back then, people were not embalmed routinely the way they are now, so you had to be put in the ground quickly.

I don't remember much about that time, just that the weather was cold and Mama's casket was black with silver handles. I had held up pretty good—Mama's death just didn't seem very real to me. But when they started to lower her casket into that cold earth, the reality of what had happened to us really struck home: I had no mama anymore. I began to cry just as hard as everyone else.

Daddy had to work, so he couldn't keep all of us together at home. We were divided among relatives, who each offered to take a couple of us. When a parent died back then, it was a common practice to split a large family up.

I went to Nashville to live with my father's brother Jerry and his wife, Joyce. They lived in a two-family house on Tenth Avenue. Aunt Joyce and Uncle Jerry lived in one part of the house with their daughter Irene. Irene was thirteen when I was born, so by the time I came to Nashville, she had finished high school, graduated from two-year college, and was teaching school.

Aunt Joyce's mother lived in the house attached to ours. She was a big, fat, white-looking woman. We called her Granny. She had been married to Aunt Joyce's father, Great-uncle Granville. He was an extremely handsome, brown-skinned man, and Joyce was the apple of his eye. Even when she was grown, she was a daddy's girl.

I never met my great-uncle Granville; he died before I moved to live with Aunt Joyce. But the family still talks about how when Uncle Granville died, Aunt Joyce put on her black mourning clothes and kept them on even after the mourning period was over. She stayed in black for the rest of her life. That's how she showed her love for her daddy.

I loved my mama, but I wasn't going to wear black for the rest of my life. Children weren't even allowed to wear black back then. If a close family member died and you were a young child, you wore lavender or deep purple or gray. Or if it was summer, white.

But I knew enough about myself, even at that young age, to know how much I liked pretty clothes! And while I would miss Mama every single day, I decided the thing to do would be to behave in a way that would make her proud when she checked up on me from Heaven.

And that did not involve dressing in black for the rest of my life.

OVERLEAF, LEFT: *Great-uncle Granville Washington, Aunt Joyce's father.*

OVERLEAF, RIGHT: *Aunt Joyce and baby Irene.* —◦❧

CHAPTER FOUR

New Life in Nashville

I MISSED MY MOTHER terribly and didn't see Daddy too much either. He was still working out on the farm, and it was hard for him to find a way to come into town. But Joyce and her husband, Jerry, were very kind to me. My cousin Irene treated me like she was my big sister, and because Irene was so sensible and levelheaded, they let me go wherever she went. They trusted her to take good care of me when she went around town. And she went around town a lot!

Irene was pretty and smart. She was teaching in the Nashville public schools for colored children, which was a little confusing to some people, because Irene was almost as fair as Aunt Joyce. A lot of people thought Aunt Joyce and her husband were white. They didn't pass for white—they just had that look.

Joyce worked for the president of Nashville's biggest bank, First National Bank. She oversaw the household staff and did a lot of errands for the family. She had her own accounts at many of the stores. All the shopkeepers knew her, so when I wanted something, I could bring it to the counter and just tell them, "Charge it to Joyce Nixon." They didn't know whether she was black or white. All they knew was that the bank president had said, "Give her what she needs," and the bills got paid on time. So they weren't going to look into matters too much.

The bank president was the first person in town to own an automobile, and he hired Daddy's and Uncle Jerry's brother, Uncle George Nixon, to be his chauffeur. But Uncle George was like everybody else—he'd never driven a car. He hadn't had the opportunity. So the president arranged for someone to come out and teach Uncle George to drive. That driver was a black man! After a while, cars became more common. We even had one in our family: Aunt Mary's husband, Will Graves, owned one.

OVERLEAF: *After my mother died, my aunt Joyce became my surrogate mother. She was very good to me. I don't know if I thought she was beautiful because she was so kind to me, or if she really was as beautiful as I remember. These pictures seem to say she was both. They were taken when she was a young woman—probably before her father died, because after that she wore black for the rest of her life. As I said earlier, back in those days, you got dressed up to have your photo taken, and the photographer often used props. These pictures were probably taken on the same day, and just involved a change of clothes. In the first one, Aunt Joyce is in her nicest summer outfit—this was at the turn of the century, and there was no such thing as short sleeves!—posed at a painted prop that looked like a garden gate. In the second one, the backdrop is winter, so Aunt Joyce is in her formal visiting outfit—a heavy coat (with a bustle in the back, which was very fashionable then) trimmed in fur, with a matching fur muff, to keep her hands warm. The hat was probably felt.* —◦⤜

Joyce knew a lot about etiquette from working in the rich white people's home. She knew which silver fork to place where and how platters should be passed to guests at the table, and what finger bowls were for and how to use them. She had a good eye, and the things in her house were as nice as the things you'd find in most white people's homes. Better, really, because some of the things she had came from her employers. They would say, "Joyce, can you use this?" and she would bring the thing to our house.

In the summer, the bank president and his family would go out to their country home in Elmwood, a little ways out. It was a big farm, really—lots of land and plenty of animals. When school was out, I would go there, too, and stay with Aunt Joyce, who oversaw everything around the huge house. About thirty servants worked under her. Aunt Joyce and Uncle Jerry had their own apartment inside the house, and I stayed there with them. There was the funniest thing on the first

---

Aunt Mary's husband, Will Graves, was one of the very few car owners in Nashville at that time. This is his car in front of our house on Tenth Avenue. I had climbed into it and sat at the wheel while someone took my picture.　—◦➤

floor in the back of the house: a big box with numbers on it. The numbers stood for a room in the house—say, the dining room was number 12. When the bank president was in the dining room and wanted something, he would press a button, and down in the back of the house the bell for number 12 would ring. That's how the servants knew what room they were needed in. It was just odd to me as a child, but years and years later, I remember seeing the same thing on television, on one of those English programs that showed the difference between life in the servants' quarters and life for the home owners. So I guess that system came to us from England. I don't know what wealthy people use now to signal their help; I haven't been in a home like that in decades.

Even before Joyce went to work for the bank president, our Nashville family had nice things. That's because Aunt Joyce's father had been a slave on Wessyngton Plantation, thirty miles north of Nashville. Aunt Joyce was born on the plantation; the family later moved to Nashville. The plantation was owned by a single family, the Washingtons, for 188 years. It still stands and is privately owned by another family, according to John Baker Jr. He interviewed me for a history he wrote of the plantation's descendants called *The Washingtons of*

Wessyngton Plantation. Aunt Joyce's father, Great-uncle Granville, was actually one of the plantation owner's children. You know how it was back then: there were the white children who were acknowledged and the colored ones everybody knew about but didn't talk about.

Before Emancipation, Granville was the valet to George Augustine Washington, or Old Master, as his slaves called him. Granville saved his master's life during the Civil War when a group of Union soldiers came to Wessyngton and shot him for killing one of their men. The man Old Master killed had stolen one of his horses. So when Old Master died, he left Uncle Granville five hundred dollars. I think Great-uncle Granville used some of that money to buy the house Aunt Joyce and Uncle Jerry were living in when I came to stay with them.

The children were also given things from the plantation: furniture, serving ware, those kinds of things. Between the antiques her father handed down from Old Master, the things that Joyce was given by her employers, and the things she bought herself, Joyce's house was full of nice things that have all been handed down to family members through the years. I have a couple myself.

Irene, an only child, was social and people liked having her around, so she would go out to parties and events and would take me with her. There I was, barely thirteen or so, and I was mixing with the grown folks. The experience made me able to talk to just about anybody about anything. When you are a good conversationalist, people want to be around you. That was true then and it's true now. I brought my children up to be able to speak to grown-ups, too. It's terrible to be seated next to a young person and all they can say is "huh?" and "uh." I am always delighted to be able to talk to young people who know a little something about current events and who are good listeners.

I learned to be a good listener. And Irene taught me to dance and play cards, so sometimes I could sit in for a hand when we went to card parties. She also counseled me on fashion. I liked seeing Mama dressed up. She made her own clothes. Aunt Joyce and Irene had their dresses made for them, or sometimes they bought them

---

This is my uncle George, Aunt Joyce's brother-in-law. Uncle George was my father's brother, and they favor each other. After my daddy died, a few years after Mama, looking at Uncle George every day was a nice way to remind me of my daddy. Uncle George was the chauffeur of an important white family in town, and this was the uniform he wore every day. —•◈

downtown. I think my interest in being well dressed started by watching Mama, but it really took off when I moved to Nashville and got to see how they dressed in the city!

I remember one spring, all us girls in high school decided we were going to wear white silk stockings with our Easter outfits. I didn't have any, of course—stockings were a real luxury back then, they cost a lot of money. The ones I wanted cost $1.75, about what you'd pay for a single scoop of ice cream today. But back then it was a small fortune, and it was going to take a heap of saving to get those stockings in time for Easter.

And save I did. Irene would give me lunch money every week from her teacher's salary. Lunch at school cost about 15 cents, I would often save some or most of that money, which meant I went hungry at lunch. Or I would have, if a group of friends hadn't taken pity on me. Several times a week, someone would offer me part of their sandwich or a piece of fruit or what have you. And that kept me going until I got home that afternoon. I'm sure Aunt Joyce was wondering what got into me to eat so much as soon as I got home *and* still be able to eat dinner, too.

Well, Easter Sunday came around and all that sacrifice had been worth it: I walked into church with my

Easter hat, my dress—and underneath it all, a pair of white silk stockings.

The State Capital

BEFORE THE FIRST World War, Nashville was a really busy city, and the black community in Nashville was impressive. In the years after freedom, a small professional class had grown up, so there were several business owners, a few doctors, dentists, and lawyers. We had our own newspaper. And many of our church congregations were active in social and civic matters. Nashville had a stable black middle class, much, much smaller than the black middle class is now. But the modest size meant that everybody knew one another.

Most of the people in my circle knew me because of Irene. I went to the same high school she'd graduated from, and I got to date boys who were a little older than the ones I went to school with because of her. Whenever a college boy from Fisk or one of the other schools was interested, he'd have to go through Irene to get to me. If she didn't say he was okay, that was that, it didn't happen. If one boy wasn't right, there was always another one right behind him.

I have to tell you, I had a lot of admirers back then. I was little—well under five feet and under one hundred pounds—but I had a womanly build. I had a really good figure—people always told me so—but I was proudest of my legs. They were great legs and still are. Fortunately for me, the style at the time called for shorter dresses, so I got to show off my legs a lot. And the young men really appreciated that.

While I was still in high school, I went to work for one of the big churches in Nashville for a few hours every day after school. Aunt Joyce didn't want me coming home to an empty house, so I'd go over to wherever Irene was working. She taught at a school that was run by a church, and she got me a job in the publishing office of the AME Sunday School Union. Back then, the biggest churches not only held services, they also

---

Me, at age seventeen. I always looked younger than my real age. That's part of the reason it took forever to convince a minister to marry us when the time came. Hard to believe someone who looked like this could have a husband and run a household—but that's what I was doing a few years later. I remember this dress very clearly—it was one of my favorites: sapphire blue satiny material and, around the neck, some cream-colored velvet tabs held on by a silk string. ———◦❧

published a lot of Christian papers, journals, and hymnal books. So I went to work for one of the publishing houses. I ended up being the best proofreader they had. I could catch an error from several feet away. It got so they would wait for me in particular to scan things before they went out. The head editor would holler, "Don't print it—Nixon found a mistake!" And they would go in and correct it, and he would give them the go-ahead. I really liked that work.

I also helped with Sunday school at Lea Chapel AME Church, and I belonged to a lot of clubs and organizations around town. I think people thought I was hardworking, but they knew I liked to have fun, too. I definitely liked to laugh. You have to be able to laugh if you're going to get through life.

So there I was, running around with lots of girlfriends, having several young men callers (when Irene okayed them), and enjoying my first steps into adult life. My life could have gone on that way for a good little while, except I went to a dance one night and everything changed.

CHAPTER FIVE

Such a Beautiful Man

M Y LIFE IN NASHVILLE was wonderful. Church offered us many activities such as concerts, picnics, and what have you. Then there were card parties. I was pretty good at cards. We were Christian, but not sanctified, so as long as we were playing just for fun, to be social and not for money, it was all right.

At some point, someone decided to form a dance class that was held on a weekend afternoon—Saturday, I think it was. Irene and I signed up to go; we loved to dance. But we also knew the dance lessons would have plenty of young men from the neighboring colleges. Here's how it worked: somebody would spend time visiting friends and family, and going to parties in several nearby cities so he could learn all the new dances. Then he'd come back and teach them to us.

This wasn't fancy ballroom dancing, mind you. These were popular dances of the day, like the foxtrot. So there we would all be, practicing and laughing at ourselves and the others. I had so much fun. I kept the dancing up until I was about one hundred five. Only then did I have to slow down after I fractured my hip.

Dancing class was where I met my husband. I was dancing away with some poor freshman from Meharry Medical College; he might was going to be a good doctor, but a good dancer? No. That poor fellow was trying to keep up with me, and all of a sudden I heard this voice say, "Move over, crab!"

The first-year students were called crabs—who knows where that came from?—by the upper classmen. So that voice had to belong to a junior or senior. I looked around and there was this good-looking man holding out his hand and asking me to dance. The crab had skittered away. He said his name was Albert Berry Cooper Jr., and he was a third-year dental student at Meharry.

Albert Berry Cooper Jr. was an eyeful, let me tell

you. He wasn't too tall, but he had a nice build, deep brown skin, and serious eyes that twinkled when he looked at me. When he smiled, I saw he had the prettiest teeth—a good thing, given his chosen career.

He was a very good dancer, thank goodness. We danced pretty much the rest of the night. Every time someone came over and asked, "May I cut in?" he would bark "No!" and they would leave. And I didn't mind one bit.

At the end of the evening, A. B.—that's what everybody called him—asked if it was all right if he called me. I said yes, and gave him my phone number. All the while I was thanking God and Uncle Jerry. Uncle Jerry, because he had put in a phone months ago. We were the only family in our neighborhood that had one at the time. When our neighbors needed to call someone, they would come to use our phone. If the call was long-distance—which usually meant it was an emergency or something important; nobody called long distance "just because" in those days—they'd leave a little money by the phone to help out with the cost.

A. B. Cooper did call, and he asked if he could come by and see me. Before long, he was a regular visitor at our house. And after a while, I stopped seeing those other admirers and was happy to have just one.

By Christmastime of that year everybody knew we were a couple. Nashville was full of holiday activities. There were parties and dances every weekend leading up to Christmas. My cousin Irene gave a Christmas party every year, and all her friends came. I invited him with Irene's permission and he accepted. And there was one big dance that everybody who was anybody was going to. I couldn't wait to go and dance with A. B. all night.

But at the last minute, he decided to go to Georgia, where he was from. He was going to see his family, but he was also going to visit with this woman he had been seeing before he left for school. She was from there as well and would be home for the Christmas holidays. She had been his girlfriend before he went off to Meharry and she went off to Kentucky for a teaching job. This lady had written A. B. at the last minute and told him she was coming home. So I think he felt obligated to her. I didn't want him to go, but I did appreciate that he felt he should. It showed good character. But I would be lying if I didn't admit I was mighty hurt.

Here was this big dance that was coming, and suddenly I wasn't going to be able to go because I wouldn't have a date. Irene told me, "Well, just go with somebody else. I know plenty of nice men who would take you." But I didn't want to go with any of them, I wanted to go with A. B.

Well, by the time the evening of the dance rolled around, I was one sad child, let me tell you. I sat in the living room by the fireplace just crying my eyes out—a little colored Cinderella. Joyce said, "You need to get on up, wipe your face, get dressed, and go to that dance. Don't let him know how much he hurt you."

The advice was sound, but I couldn't take it. I was too sad. So I just cried so hard I was hiccupping.

It was late, and Irene was getting ready to go upstairs to bed. I think she had lost patience with my boo-hooing a couple of hours before that. Suddenly, the doorbell rang. You should have seen my head whip up—like a puppy when it hears the postman coming! Something told me I would want to see who was on the other side of the door. I wiped my eyes, went to the door, and who was there, but my A. B.! He hadn't gone away after all. He had put that woman aside in favor of me. I had never seen such a beautiful man as A. B. looked that night, standing on the front porch.

We fell into each other's arms and never fell out again. That was our first and only disagreement; we really were inseparable after that. Now we were a couple

---

and neither of us saw anybody else. I have no idea what happened to the Kentucky schoolteacher.

We didn't get to the dance that night and we didn't mind. We just sat by the fireplace, holding hands, and dreaming about the future that we knew we were going to have together. Me and my beautiful man.

Albert Berry Cooper Jr. at age eighteen. Even then he was a serious young man! ——◦≫

CHAPTER SIX

Mrs. A. B. Cooper Jr.

B ACK IN OUR DAY, when you got serious about someone, it was understood that you were going to be
married sooner or later.

We wanted to be married sooner. A. B. would graduate from Meharry, and from there, he was going to go
wherever he could get a job. We had no idea where that
would be. We wanted to be married in time for me to
go with him.

Plenty of young people back then got married far
earlier than they do now. There wasn't a bunch of years
of dating, and nice girls certainly didn't just go off and

live with their young men. You did things in a certain order: you met someone, you kept company, you got engaged, then you got married, and *then* you started having children. That's just how it was, and that's not a bad thing. It kept relationships stable and made men responsible to their families.

Things have changed a lot. I know because every now and then when I'm out, I like to stop into the grocery store or the bookstore. Seems like every other magazine I see has young girls—of all colors—pregnant as they are planning their weddings. Some are Hollywood stars who you would think would want to set a good example for their fans and followers, but maybe I'm old-fashioned. I guess it's not such a big deal now as back when I was a young woman. But I still think it's a bad idea to have the baby before the marriage. If Aunt Joyce were alive to see all these babies-before-the-weddings today, she would have had a flat-out fit. So back then a lot of people did get married young so they could be together without causing a scandal. A. B. was twenty-two years old when we got together; he was considered an adult. But I was barely twenty and would need the permission of a responsible adult. I didn't ask Irene, because she'd gotten married to a dentist by then— a Meharry man who was living in the house with us.

He wasn't old enough to be my father, but he certainly did boss me around like he was my daddy. He had very definite thoughts about what I should and shouldn't be doing—what kinds of dresses I should be wearing, who I should be seeing. I didn't want him to put his two cents in about whether and when I could get married.

I wanted a quiet little wedding ceremony, not something fancy with the whole town looking on. That wasn't for me. Graduation was coming up, and I knew we needed to decide what we were going to do. Otherwise there was a chance that we would be separated for who knows how long. Before graduation, A. B. took me to a photographer and had photographs made for us. One was of me for him to take, and one was of him and me for me to keep. It's one of my favorites still. You can see that we both liked to dress well, even when we were young and didn't have anything much.

A. B.'s daddy made the trip to Nashville to see him graduate. We were all so proud. And while he was there, he talked to a friend he knew, a black newspaperman, to see if he could help A. B. out. As a consequence, the newspaperman vouched for A. B. to a new Atlanta bank, Citizen's Trust, and they gave him a loan to start his practice.

So he went off to Atlanta, thinking that would be

a good place for a young professional man to grow a business. Atlanta was a bigger city than Nashville, so it could use more than one black doctor or dentist. He made me promise to write him every single day, and I said I would. I am a faithful letter writer. I wrote long letters to my friends and family for several decades, on special paper that was almost a yard long. They used to sell it in stationery stores (there used to *be* way more stationery stores than there are today). Nobody writes like that anymore.

We figured we might be able to marry by Christmas 1922, but once he left for Atlanta, I didn't hear from A. B. for weeks, not a word. Then I got a phone call full of good news. He had started his practice, and he'd done a lot of work already. So much work, he'd reached his goal ahead of time: "I made $500 this month, so we don't have to wait until Christmas to get married!" Well, that was just fine by me. I was already tired of being separated.

We knew a nice pastor, Reverend Ellis, and we visited him to ask if he would consider marrying us. We had to ask a number of times, because he kept saying no. Reverend Ellis thought I was too young to marry. "Just wait a bit," he'd tell us. "No need to rush; wait until you're a little older."

Well, that was easy for *him* to say—he'd been married for years. So I went back several times with several different arguments aimed at convincing Reverend Ellis I really was mature enough to marry.

He took some convincing. A lot of people thought I was younger than I was because I was so little, and I had a kind of bubbly personality. I laughed a lot, but that didn't mean I didn't take things seriously. I'd been working for two years, and I was mature and sensible, even if I was only four foot ten inches tall. I think eventually Reverend Ellis came around because he saw I had good sense and because A. B. seemed levelheaded. He was not one of those boys who would promise to marry you just to have his way with you. He was honorable.

So he came back to Nashville for a few days so we could marry. One evening, I told Irene I was going out for a bit and would be back in a little while. She didn't worry about it. I went out and about on my own fairly often. But I really went a few blocks away and met A. B. I was wearing a nice dress—but not so nice as to arouse anyone's suspicions—and A. B. had on a good suit. We walked over to Reverend Ellis's house, and we were married in his parlor with Mrs. Ellis as our witness. Reverend Ellis made us promise to be good to each other, and we were happy to make that pledge.

So on July 11, 1922, I went in the Ellises' door as Ann Louise Nixon, and I came out of it Mrs. A. B. Cooper Jr. I was ecstatic.

Then we went home to break the news to Irene and her husband.

Irene was pretty happy about us. We had cheated her out of a wedding, but we avoided all the fuss and anxiety a wedding often produces.

I think also that Irene was happy to have me settled down, because there were always boys coming to the door—even when I told them I wasn't available because I was seeing A. B. exclusively. Now A. B. and I could be together all the time with no problem. We sent a telegram to A. B.'s father and mother. He was a minister and pretty strict, but Daddy Cooper and I would eventually become good friends.

A. B. went back to Atlanta to find a home for the two of us and to do some more work. I planned to join him in a few weeks.

He was ready by the end of the summer, and he sent me a train ticket. I would leave for Atlanta on Labor Day weekend. "Don't tarry getting on the train," A. B. told me, "and don't talk to anybody on the ride down. Just keep to yourself and watch for me on the platform. I'll be waiting."

And that's what I did. I had a few books to read during the ride. I might speak to the ladies as they passed, but I didn't say anything to the men. I knew how jealous A. B. would be if he thought I was striking up conversations with them. Not that he needed to tell me anything. I was only interested in one man, and he was in Atlanta waiting for me.

Finally, the train pulled into the station. I stood up, trying to get the wrinkles out of my dress. I checked my hair in my little compact and refreshed my lipstick. I pulled my hat down just so, the way he liked it, and then I started looking out the window.

At first I didn't see anyone, and I wondered if A. B. had forgotten he was supposed to meet me. There were plenty of people on the platform, but I didn't see my groom.

Then, just as I was starting to get anxious and my heart started beating fast, I saw him. He was running toward the train, waving and smiling. That made me smile, too. The Pullman porter helped me with my train case, down the steps and into my new husband's arms.

And Dr. and Mrs. Albert Berry Cooper Jr. went off to start their new life in Atlanta.

CHAPTER SEVEN

"The Cutest Thing I Have Ever Seen"

A B. HAD FOUND a room for us on Davis Street (it exists today, but it's now called Northside Drive) in the home of a man I'll call Dr. X and his wife. We had one bedroom and kitchen privileges. The arrangement was lovely at first, but I quickly realized that I needed something to do with myself while A. B. spent hours at work every day. As it was, I ended up staring at the four walls, waiting for lunchtime, so I could at least go down to the kitchen and sit in a different room for a minute. I had had satisfying work and a full social life in Nashville. Now here I was in a strange city, in a strange house, living with strangers and having nothing to do. Well, *that* wasn't good.

It took some time to convince A. B. that me working would be a good thing for both of us. I'd have something productive to do with my time, and we would be able to buy our own home that much sooner, something we both wanted.

Most married women didn't work outside the home in those days; they stayed in and took care of their husbands, children, and the house. A. B. relented—very reluctantly, I can tell you—and I went off in search of work.

I found a job very quickly. A lot of black-owned businesses were setting up to serve people that the other big downtown businesses wouldn't. Atlanta Life was one of them and happened to be the city's biggest insurance company. It was owned and run by the Herndon family, who would become our dear friends in a few years. But I didn't know that then. I just knew the company

Me and Daddy.

was hiring: secretaries, stenographers, policy writers, you name it. And a lot of the employees were women.

So I went to work at Atlanta Life, at first as a secretary. I knew Gregg shorthand and could write quickly and accurately. But then they discovered I had very nice handwriting, so they put me to work as a policy writer. If the old records are around for policies from the early days, you can see how beautiful my handwriting was.

The work didn't pay a whole lot by today's standards—maybe five or six dollars a week—but it was money nonetheless. Having the job got me out of the house for the day and introduced me to some of Atlanta's young ladies who were my age.

The Herndons were Atlanta's upper crust, and many of the young women they employed came from similar families. They'd been to or were attending Spelman, the exclusive women's college on the Atlanta University (AU) campus. Or they attended one of the other schools in the AU Center complex—Clark and Morehouse colleges, the graduate school at the time, Atlanta University, and Morris Brown College. Their boyfriends went to one of those schools or, most usually, Morehouse College, the brother school to Spelman. Morehouse and Spelman were considered elite institutions, and the students who went there were justifiably proud of having gotten in. Two of my girls would eventually graduate from Spelman.

So the Atlanta Life Insurance office was populated with these elegant girls from important families who all knew each other. And then there was me—who nobody knew. All they knew was that I was newly married to a man who had been one of the town's most eligible bachelors. The fact that this handsome professional man could have married one of them was not lost on them. So while they were all polite (as you can imagine, it wouldn't do for a Spelman girl to be thought rude), they were definitely interested in finding out more about this little nobody who had married one of "their" men.

"Where did you go to school?" they'd ask. "Maybe we have friends in common." I would then have to explain that I hadn't gone to college, which of course is what they wanted me to say out loud. They thought I would find that embarrassing, but I didn't. While I'd wanted to go to college, I knew it would be expensive. So I went to work right out of high school, as a lot of girls did. I didn't see any shame in it.

"How did you meet your husband?" So I'd tell them the story of meeting A. B. That wasn't enough for some of them. I distinctly remember one girl saying to me in the lunchroom, "I don't get it—you're not even pretty!"

She, on the other hand, was quite pretty. I shrugged it off and acted like it didn't bother me, but my feelings were hurt.

I'd never been told I was beautiful, but in Nashville I'd been considered quite good-looking.

I thought about that "not pretty" remark all the way home. When A. B. came home, he noticed I was kind of quiet.

"What's wrong?" he asked.

"I want to ask you something, and I want you to tell me the truth," I told him.

He straightened up and gave me his full attention. "Okay, I'm listening."

I took a deep breath. "Do you think I'm pretty?"

"Why do you ask me if you're pretty?"

"Well, the girls at work said they thought you'd marry a girl prettier than me."

He frowned at me and then he started shaking his head. In a minute he was laughing out loud, showing that beautiful smile.

—A wife and a mother! This is me with our first baby, Gwendolyn Yvonne. She had grown a LOT in eight weeks! After Gwen's birth, I started calling A. B. Daddy, and he called me Mother. And that's what we did until he died.

"Well, I never thought about *pretty*," A. B. said, as he got up from his chair and put his arms around my waist. "But you," he said slowly, looking right in my eyes, "are the *cutest* thing I have ever seen."

"Really?"

"The." And he kissed me on one cheek.

"Cutest." The other cheek.

"Thing." Lips.

So that settled that. If A. B. thought I was cute, I really didn't care what my coworkers thought. I came back to work with a lighter heart and never worried about who—besides my husband, of course—thought what.

I enjoyed my work and I really enjoyed being able to contribute to the household income. Those small amounts I earned started to add up. Which was a good thing, because Dr. X and his wife were giving us ample inspiration to move. (Now you'll see why I don't call him by name.) They fought—verbally and *physically*—several times a week. You could hear them screaming at each other—well, truth be told, it was mostly him screaming at her—all through the night. It drove A. B. crazy. We tolerated the situation until I got pregnant.

"That's it," A. B. said. "We have to find a house." He didn't want his children brought into the world in Dr. X's house, and neither did I.

———

They were building new houses over on Mayson Turner Road and we bought one of those. And that was where we were living when the children were born. Gwendolyn Yvonne Cooper, our first child, was born in 1924. We found her name in a magazine A. B.'s cousin brought to us and thought it sounded beautiful. Then came Joyce Nixon Cooper in 1925, who was named after my dear aunt Joyce. Albert Berry Cooper III arrived in 1929 was named for his father and grandfather, and Ann Marie Cooper, born in 1932, was named after me and my dear friend Marie Brown. Marie's husband was E. Franklin Frazier, who was at that point the dean of the School of Social Work at Atlanta University.

Before the children arrived, my husband and I called each other by our first names. But almost as soon as I became pregnant, "Ann" gave way to "Mother" and "A. B." became "Daddy." And that is how we referred to each other from then on.

Gwen and Joyce were born in a home one of the city's black doctors rented and used as a clinic. This happened out of necessity. If you were black, you could not go to the white hospitals in Atlanta to have your baby. You could go to the doctor's offices to be seen, but if he had white patients, you had to wait out in the hallway or on the porch. What a terrible state of things.

———

I remember taking Gwen to see a specialist because she was having trouble breathing—the result, the doctor said, of being born in that unheated home clinic. Well, while at the doctor's we were made to stand outside in the hall. Here I was with this young baby who couldn't breathe very well, and we were left to wait in this drafty hall. When I finally got inside, I saw that he had a colored assistant, and I gave her what-for about the wait. "I am not coming back here to stand in anybody's hall," I told her. "You remind your employer that his services have already been paid for!" This was before health insurance existed. If you needed to see the doctor, you paid for it in full, often before he even saw you. So this doctor, who already had my money in his pocket, was treating us like this.

The assistant was embarrassed, but she couldn't do anything about it. That's how things were back then.

Shortly after that, I ran into Dr. C. W. Powell, a family friend who had delivered Gwen and Joyce. I told him I was through having babies in anybody's house.

A. B. stands with our completed family: Ann Marie, Gwen, A. B. III, and Joyce. That's Daddy's Model T.

"You need to build a hospital so colored women can have their babies in safety and comfort," I told him. He smiled and told me he'd take that suggestion "under advisement."

But don't you know, that's just what he did. By 1928, William A. Harris Memorial Hospital, named for Mrs. Powell's father, was up and running, and my two youngest children, A. B. III and Ann Marie, were born there. To this day, when we pass by it, my family refers to it as "the hospital they built so you could have your babies." And it's true. Mine and a lot of others beside. Nowadays, you can go anywhere you want to have your child delivered, but those of us who remember when we had no hospital are very grateful to Dr. Powell and his family, who gave us a good, safe place to have our babies.

CHAPTER EIGHT

"Meet Me at Rich's"

Life was full at the house on Mayson Turner Road. Daddy had a thriving practice, the children were busy with school and other activities, and black Atlanta kept growing and growing.

We knew we would need a bigger home as the children grew older, and Daddy swore the next time we moved, it would be to someplace that had a lot of land. The houses on Mayson Turner Road were too close together for his taste. We thought we'd escaped listening to domestic knockdowns when we left Dr. X and his wife, but soon discovered that at least one of our neighbors now had the same unfortunate habit of beating his wife. Unlike poor Mrs. X, who mostly took the beatings, one of our current neighbors decided to retaliate. When her husband came home ready to beat on her one day, she killed him dead with a butcher knife in their own kitchen. We heard her call her mother on the phone and tell her to call the police to have them remove the body! That was a little *too* much excitement for us.

Daddy was determined to live somewhere where he couldn't hear the neighbors talk to each other, let alone fight. So he told me to start looking for a house.

I knew that if he wanted the house to be surrounded by land, it was going to have to be a new house, farther from the center of town. So I would take the trolley out as far as it would go on Hunter and peek at the new homes going up. Word was that after the railroad trestle crossed Hunter, the street became white. But a few black families were quietly buying homes in the area, so I didn't see why we couldn't do the same.

One of our friends told us about a new home that had just been built and was going to be put on the market. Apparently, the man who had asked that it be built thought it cost too much when it was finished. He didn't want to or couldn't afford to pay for it, so

it was going to just sit there. Daddy and I went out to take a look.

"Like it?" he asked me after we went through it.

"Love it!"

"We'll take it," Daddy told the Realtor, "on one condition: you have to sell me the lots on either side and in back of the house."

Well, as you can imagine, the Realtor didn't mind that at all. So Daddy finally had his privacy, and he enjoyed every minute of it.

In 1938 we moved in. Daddy had navy blue sun awnings installed with our initial inside a big crest "so

---

Daddy and I liked to travel when we could, and we often went to New York, for the theater, and shopping, and to visit friends. In this picture, we're in Club Zanzibar, in Manhattan in 1946. It was all decked out in an African Safari theme— see the cheetah fabric on the banquette behind us?—and there were beautiful girls circulating with trays of cigarettes for the customers. The ones that didn't have cigarettes wandered around with cameras. Daddy let one of the photo girls take a picture of us (you can see the flash in the mirror behind us), and he bought one to take home. I'm so glad he did, because it's one of the few photos I have of him where he's halfway smiling. —∘⟫

you'll know which house is yours," he joked. They were the same kind he had on one side of his office in town. Daddy planted hedges all along the long driveway and flower beds all around the house. It was a beautiful sight.

The new house on Hunter was bigger than the previous one, on Mayson Turner Road, and Daddy encouraged me to fill it with whatever I wanted. "You're the boss," he said.

We had a great time deciding on furniture, linens, and things. On Fridays, Daddy would often call from the office. "I'll be finished in a few hours," he'd tell me. "If you can come to town, meet me at Rich's, and we'll do a little looking around."

Rich's was the big department store in town, with all kinds of lovely things. Daddy knew I loved to shop down there—even window shop. So I'd put on a nice dress, walk down the street to catch the trolley, and meet him at Rich's. We'd look at things for the house and sometimes buy something, sometimes not. It was just nice to have that time together alone, to relax at the end of a long week. Friday nights were what I guess you would call our "date night"—just me and Daddy. Those were wonderful evenings.

Back then, women had difficulty getting charge accounts in their own names, but if your husband didn't mind, you could get one in your own name. Daddy was fine with me having an account to get whatever I thought we needed, so I applied for a charge account at Rich's. The store would give me one, but only if it said Ann Cooper—no "Mrs.," like they did for the white women. I wanted the same courtesy. So when I first applied for an account, they asked me who it was for and in what name it should be. I would tell them the card should be in my name: "Mrs. A. B. Cooper" or "Mrs. Ann Cooper." Well, the lady in the credit department didn't want to call a black woman "Mrs." Anything, so we'd go around and around: "What's the A for? What's the B for?" *None of her business, is what!* It took several weeks, but eventually I got my card the way I wanted it, and when I charged things after that, they were charged to *Mrs.* Ann Cooper.

OVERLEAF, LEFT: *A more formal portrait of the Cooper family, taken in our living room. Daddy sits with Ann Marie on his lap, Joyce is next to her, Gwen (starting to look quite grown!) is next to Joyce, and the baby, A. B., is next to me. Everybody but Joyce looks deathly serious—I have no idea why! (And don't you know, I still have that dress. And can fit into it!)*

OVERLEAF, RIGHT: *Our 1948 custom-made Packard. Daddy insisted that those big whitewalls be kept spotless!*   —◦➧

(I have kept my Rich's card over the years. A little over six years ago, I went down to the store to buy a new sofa for the den. The young man who waited on me gave me an extra discount because when he went back to look up my account, it turned out that nobody with a Rich's card had one longer than I have. That was wonderful, but I had to ask him about buying the stain-repellent guarantee: it's good for five years, and I'm sure he didn't offer it because he figured I wouldn't be around for the whole time. Joke's on him: that warranty ran out last year, and I'm still here. So I got my money's worth.)

Daddy liked buying things for the house about as much as I did. We were driving back from a trip to Nashville once, and while the car was stopped at a light, I saw a beautiful cut-glass lamp in a shop window. Daddy drove on, but in a minute he said, "Did you like that lamp?"

"It's gorgeous," I told him.

My portrait at age forty, in 1942. Not bad for a middle-aged housewife and mother! The dress I'm wearing is black silk georgette, encrusted with seed pearls, semi-precious stones, and embroidered in gold thread. I loved it so much I have never thrown it away. Sally found it a few months ago and hung it on the living room wall. "It's art," she said. And I kind of agree. It tickles me just to look at it. —•➤

"Want it?"

Before I could even say, "Well, yes," he had made a U-turn and headed back to the store. The lamp was in our living room for years—you can see it in the girls' wedding photos—and later I moved it to the music room. It sits on our baby grand piano to this day, and it's one of my favorite pieces in the house.

That piano is the reason I went back to work for a little while.

Daddy assumed, of course, that once the children were born, I would stay home and not hold down a paying job. That was my intention, too, but when they got a little older, I wanted them all to take piano lessons. In order to do that, we needed a piano. And a place to put it as well.

So I told Daddy I was going to go back to work for a little while, just to make enough to add a music room onto the house. He earned a very good living, but I didn't think it fair that he had to pay for everything. He worked hard enough for us, and the music room was something I wanted, not something I had to have. So I thought I should go out and make the money to get my music room.

Well, Daddy fussed and fussed, but he also realized that I was ultimately going to have my way, so he gave

Joyce's wedding photo. You can see the lamp in the background.

—◦❧

his consent. And for about a year I went back to Atlanta Life. But now I wasn't the New Girl from Nashville—I was a well-established Atlantan, married to one of the city's most prominent professional men. We were now friends with the Herndons, the company's founders. There was no reason for me not to spend a few hours a day in the policy department while the children were in school. And it was worth it. I got my grand piano. I picked one out—a beautiful dark-wood model—and had the room built around it. Literally.

Once the money was in place, we had the windows at the end of the dining room removed, the wall knocked down, and two new walls built. Then they brought the piano in and put it in place before the final wall went up.

Now when you sat in the dining room, you had a view through a big archway of our baby grand piano in front of the newly placed windows. All the children did take music lessons, though none of them played profession-

---

Being married for twenty years called for a celebration, so we had a fancy party in our new home to mark the occasion. A photographer came to the house to snap the Coopers in their fancy dress, ready to receive their guests. (Left to right) Ann Marie, A. B. III, Joyce, Gwen, me, and Daddy. Don't we look nice? I was forty years old, Daddy was forty-two.

---

ally. I hoped Gwen might become a classical pianist, but she wanted to be a doctor. Nevertheless, I still love that room, which we have used a lot over the years. We always hired someone to play when we had dinner parties. And there was always a professional pianist there when I hosted my club meetings—usually it was Dr. G. Johnson Hubert. He was the chairman of the music department at Morris Brown University, and a well-known musician. But he was also a dear friend who was kind enough to provide us with lovely music for many social events. We also had guests who played beautifully and often treated us to an impromptu concert.

One such guest was Nat "King" Cole, who came to town with his new bride, Maria Ellington Cole. (She was not related to Duke Ellington, although at one point she sang with his band.) We had not met the Coles previously, but we knew Maria's aunt, Miss Charlotte Hawkins Brown. Miss Brown ran the most exclusive black boarding school in the country: Palmer Memorial Institute, in Sedalia, North Carolina. Back before the Second World War, the South had many boarding schools for black children. If you were a black child, especially one living out in the country, often the public

Nat "King" Cole and Maria Ellington Cole.   —◦➤

schools stopped halfway through elementary school. The state felt that colored children didn't need much education; the assumption was that our children were destined for a lifetime of work as servants or field hands, so why waste the money? But many black families felt that education was going to be the way for future generations to prosper and thrive, so they made great sacrifices to send their children to these schools so they could go beyond the basics to learn things such as literature, history, and Latin. Most of these schools have faded away, but in its day, Palmer was one of the best.

My youngest children, A. B. III and Ann Marie, attended Palmer, so we came to know Miss Brown quite well. She was an extremely proper lady and insisted that her students be proper and well educated. Although these schools, including Palmer, were boarding schools, they were not what we think of today when you use the term; they weren't fancy. I remember when Ann Marie and A. B. III came home for one of their first visits, we were all having breakfast. It was the same kind of breakfast we normally had—ham or sausage and bacon and

---

←∘— Nat "King" Cole and his bride, Maria, stopped to visit with us when Nat came to Atlanta to perform. They're standing in our den, on their way to a party at Club Ann.

---

eggs and grits and fruit and hot rolls. You would have thought those children hadn't eaten for weeks! Ann Marie told me, between mouthfuls, "I never knew how luxurious my life was till we went away! I didn't realize many people don't eat as well as we do here—things like roasts and lamb chops." So living away from home taught A. B. and Ann Marie more than just Latin. It taught them to be grateful for their father's hard work that had provided them with such a pleasant life.

Attitudes were different back then. Professional people didn't necessarily mix with "show people." Entertainers were, as a group, far less conservative in their behavior and dress than other folk, and entertainment wasn't considered a completely respectable profession—at least not until the late '50s. But Miss Brown had raised Maria in much the same way Aunt Joyce had raised me, so we knew it would be fine to have the Coles over.

Since Atlanta was still racially segregated, even nationally famous entertainers like Nat Cole were forbidden to stay in the downtown hotels. If there was no colored hotel in a city or town, black entertainers had to rely on a network of friends, relatives, and others to put them up and feed them.

We knew that after a show, the artists usually want to relax and wind down. So Daddy and I decided to have the Coles and a few people who'd enjoy meeting them over for drinks and a late supper. I have a picture of Nat and Maria in our living room, taken as they were on their way to "Club Ann" to spend the evening with us and our friends. Before they left, they signed our guest book. Our guest books over the years have had a lot of famous names in them. It's fun to watch my grandchildren's eyes get big as they turn the pages.

OVERLEAF, TOP LEFT: *The exterior of Club Ann. A. B. and I loved to entertain, but I wasn't so fond of the aftermath of the entertaining—having to put the house back together! So a few years after we bought the Hunter Avenue home, he built a little house in the back just for entertaining. It had a full bar and a dance floor. Daddy christened it Club Ann. We had loads of fun in there! And when the children became old enough to entertain their friends, we let them borrow it.*

OVERLEAF, BOTTOM LEFT: *Daddy behind the bar at Club Ann.*

OVERLEAF, RIGHT: *A. B. III is behind the bar, preparing to serve Ann Marie and her boyfriend-of-the-moment. (Clearly I wasn't in the room or Miss Cooper would not have had that cigarette in her hand!)* —•❧

CHAPTER NINE

Rights and Responsibilities

E VERY NOW AND THEN, I hear somebody on one of the television shows talk about how much better life was in the black community during segregation, and I just roll my eyes and think, That's because it wasn't *you* who was waiting in a cold hallway for the doctor to see your child. It wasn't *you* who couldn't get a sandwich at a lunch counter or use the ladies' room in a department store where you'd just spent your money.

Those people are romanticizing segregation. But let me tell you something: they are right about one aspect of it. It *does* seem as if black folk back then were much more interested in helping each other out. Maybe because if we didn't help us, nobody else would.

Nashville might have been smaller than Atlanta, but in some ways, it was easier to be black there. Atlanta was burned to the ground by Sherman's army during the Civil War. Nashville, on the other hand, was left whole as a city. Huge parts of it didn't have to be rebuilt, as was the case in Atlanta. Consequently, I think the attitudes of whites toward blacks in Georgia were more hardened and harsh.

Nashville's white people weren't hardly going to let us eat at their lunch counters any more than Atlanta's for example, but they tended to be more tolerant when it came to mixing and access in one-on-one situations. My aunt Joyce, for instance, shopped in stores that didn't allow black people through the door. But because she worked for a bank president—and maybe because they were never completely sure of her racial identity with her being so fair—they just let her go on and do what she needed to do. That would not have happened in Atlanta.

Even sixty years later, Atlanta's white people were still feeling the effect of what Southern loyalists tended to call "the War Between the States." Daddy, the Georgia native, used to always warn me, "These aren't Nash-

OVERLEAF, LEFT: *"Sweet Auburn" was the backbone of Atlanta's black community for ages. You had arrived if your business or practice or church was on the street. Daddy's office was on the second floor of the Oddfellows' Building. You can see the sign for Citizens' Bank & Trust—the bank that gave Daddy his start—behind Big Bethel AME Church. Big Bethel was one of the city's biggest churches, and occupied a prominent place on Sweet Auburn.*

OVERLEAF, RIGHT: *Another view of Daddy's office. It was above the Yates & Milton Pharmacy, which was owned by family friends. You can see the awnings with the same "C" that used to hang above our windows at home (before I changed them!). And if you look up, you can see the grids that the streetcars ran on, which correspond to the metal tracks inlaid in the street. Now Atlanta has a subway system called MARTA, but the trolleys are long gone.* ⟶•❯

ville whites. These are *crackers!*" A cracker, to our way of thinking, was a poor white person who had only his whiteness to hold above black folks—and they really used it to try to keep us down. That would change in the '60s, not only in Atlanta, but also in many other places around the country. And by the 1970s, Atlanta would become one of the first big Southern cities to have a black mayor. Maynard Jackson, the son of old family friends, was elected mayor in 1973. In the 1920s up until the early '60s, however, black city leadership at that level was just not something that was hoped for.

Our children went to segregated day schools and boarding schools. The teachers these schools employed were often excellent, though, so our children didn't miss getting good educations. It isn't as if a black teacher had options for employment. The schools for white students wouldn't have them. Black professionals in education and children had so fewer options then as far as schools and extracurricular activities are concerned. When A. B. III was growing up, we wanted to put him in the Boy Scouts.

During the war, many families joined in opening their homes to entertain troops who were stationed near Atlanta. Here, a group of injured soldiers, and the medical staff that treated them, came out for an afternoon of sun and food. —⊶❧

Both Daddy and I liked their emphasis on good values and responsibility and their ability to teach useful skills, like camping, trailblazing, and what have you. But the organization was not so open to black youth then. At least, not open to having integrated troops.

So as another dear friend, the former U.S. ambassador and civil rights activist Andrew Young likes to say, quoting his mother, we had to "make a way out of no way." I wrote to the Boy Scout headquarters, told them what the situation was, and asked to how to get a troop started. They sent back information, and I called a couple of friends with children A. B.'s age and asked if they'd join. They all said yes, and called a few of

---

❦——*We thought the morals and discipline young boys got from being Boy Scouts was important, but apparently the Boy Scouts thought it was important for white boys and not ours. So I wrote to them and told them we needed Boy Scout activities for our boys, too, and what did I need to do to get that started? They send back a letter with instructions, and a few weeks later, Troop 95 was established. It became Atlanta's first black Boy Scout Troop, and it exists to this very day. In this picture, the new troop leader is explaining to the children what they will be reading in the* Handbook for Boys. *My son, A. B. III, is second from the bottom right.*

---

their friends, and soon we had enough boys to start the Cub Scouts. We were Troop 95, Atlanta's first all-black Scout troop.

I was the first den mother; I worked with those little boys for four years, and after me other mothers stepped in as new Cubs joined. Then, when the original Cubs went to the next level to become Scouts, some of the fathers stepped in to be scoutmasters. They took the boys on camping trips, collected canned goods for hungry families, and decorated the graves of colored veterans on Memorial Day, the Fourth of July, and Armistice Day (you call it Veteran's Day today). We got a citation a few years ago for starting that troop.

And we didn't want to neglect the girls, either. We felt especially responsible to girls from families that were not well-off: we knew they needed to be exposed to how to do things correctly, how to participate in community service, and how to set their sights on college if they wanted to go. You have to put those things in children's minds early. So I helped to found the Girls Club Guild of Atlanta. I became its second president and served on

---

Twelve-year-old A. B. poses with a new bicycle he won in a contest. I don't remember what for, but I do remember how proud and pleased he was. I think it's a Schwinn. ⟶✎

its auxiliary for many, many years in whatever capacity they needed me. And I'm very proud to say it still exists to this very day!

Way before there was Operation Head Start, we wanted to give the youngest children in our community a head start, so we founded the Gate City Nursery Association. Our job was to find good preschool teachers who could start these children out with good habits at their earliest age so they'd be ready for the next step. Many of these children had single mothers or mothers who worked. There wasn't a lot of that when we first started, but of course, single and working mothers became more common as time moved on. We considered the amount of time children had to be away from their mothers and understood that they needed more than just babysitting. So they learned their ABCs, how to count, and how to be nice to each other—something that some grown-ups could stand a refresher course in.

I'm sure I was busier doing all this than I would be if I'd had a paying job, but I didn't mind. It's important to contribute to your community. And back then, I think more was expected of people than it is now. We really need to promote the value of volunteering and doing community work that we once held so high. Just because the white people didn't allow us in their Scout troops, their clubs, and nursery schools didn't mean we had to go without. We were intent on making things better for ourselves—and we did that in my household and community for several decades.

Don't be putting a halo on me for doing these things. I had plenty of time to enjoy myself, too. When I first got to Atlanta, I joined the Pollyanna Bridge Club and played regularly until the Second World War. I also helped to begin a second club, the Jovial Coterie Bridge Club. (Don't ask me where that name came from, I couldn't tell you.)

I joined the Utopian Literary Club in 1948. We met once a month to discuss current events and articles in magazines and newspapers. They often came to my house because my living room was big enough to hold all the members. We would often invite guest speakers or people to lead a discussion on the topic we'd chosen. Jovial Coterie is still going on. I'm not as active as I once was, since I broke my hip. But I still like to drop in every now and again. I started or helped to start several book clubs, too, where we would read and discuss popular literature of the day. I like to say I started book clubs from one end of town to the other, and some of those are still going strong.

———

I am proud to be a charter member of Atlanta's chapter of The Links, Inc., a national organization for black women that relies on bonds (or links) of friendship to provide social service to our communities' chapters of the national organization—all the locals must be chartered by the national. We were mostly the wives of professional men, because back then, we had the time to devote to social organizations. Coretta Scott King was one of our members.

Today the Atlanta chapter is full of powerful professional women. Many are married to professional men, but they are also powerful in their *own* right. Some of the city's most prominent doctors, lawyers, and professors are members, as are many high-profile businesswomen. Our mayor, Shirley Franklin, is a Link.

I started attending First Congregational Church, one of Atlanta's oldest and finest churches, shortly after I arrived in Atlanta. I began going with Dr. X's wife. Eventually Daddy joined me, and we have been there ever since. A few years ago, when the church celebrated

---

The Atlanta chapter of The Links, Inc. That's me in the middle and Gwen, wearing the flower brooch, seated in front of me. Gwen was inducted at this meeting.

the one hundred forty-fifth anniversary of its founding, it also honored me for my many years of membership and service. It was a rare Sunday when we couldn't be found sitting in the Cooper pew, as it came to be known. I always sat in the middle aisle to the right, about five rows from the front of the church, so it became known as "our" pew. Even if we were late—which rarely happened, because Daddy didn't tolerate tardiness—the pew would remain empty until some Coopers arrived.

I wore a hat every Sunday, as most women did until the late 1960s, when mores changed. Even now, when so much else has changed, I just couldn't imagine not wearing a hat to church. I felt incomplete without one. So I had them for every season, and every Sunday I would take one out and finish my outfit.

I belonged to the church Missionary Circle, which raised money for Christian missions in foreign countries, mostly African and Caribbean countries. And a couple of times during the year, I would have a hat party. After church, all the ladies would come over to our house for tea, wearing their hats—some of them quite magnificent. We would use the occasion to raise contributions to the Missionary Fund.

I continued volunteering even after Atlanta became desegregated because, frankly, I thought the city needed my help. So I tutored people who read poorly, if at all, at Ebenezer Baptist Church, where our friend Daddy King and his son M. L. had been pastors. I did this in the late '70s, after M. L. had died and Daddy King had retired. And I've worked for years on the Friends of the Library Board, which is an organization that serves all of Atlanta.

I was helping myself while I was helping others. I learned over the years that keeping busy keeps you young. You have to take care of your spirit and mind as well as your body if you want to age well.

OVERLEAF: *I belonged to several social and civic organizations in Atlanta. This was a meeting of the Atlanta chapter of The Links, Inc., an important women's social group of which I was a charter member. It was taken at a member's home in the midsixties. I am seated on the floor, on the left (with the flower brooch). Three women away from me is Coretta Scott King; our family and the Kings had been close for many, many years. This is a rare shot of Coretta doing something fun.* —◦❥

CHAPTER TEN

Faith Will Get You Through

D ADDY AND I WORKED hard work for many years. So once he reached his late sixties and the children were grown and well established with their own families and careers, we looked forward to his retirement and spending time together.

He was a good husband, always surprising me with something here and there. His friends would tease him, often saying, "You need to stop. You're spoiling her." He didn't pay them any mind and continued

to treat me grandly. And I don't mind telling you, I loved it.

When I turned sixty-five, in 1967, A. B. and I decided to mark that milestone with friends by taking a trip to Trinidad. The National Dental Association was meeting there that year. I was really looking forward to a change of climate and how nice it would be to be able to walk at the water's edge in January. I went about preparing: packing and setting up the house for the time we'd be away. I began having the furniture covered and the rooms closed off until we got back.

The day before we went, Daddy had to see a few patients. He came into my room, as always, and pointed to a patch of sunlight that hit my wall. He said the same thing he did every morning: "See, darling? The sun came up just for you again." That always made me laugh. Then he kissed me and said, "I'll see you later."

A rare portrait of four generations of A. B. Coopers: Daddy's daddy, Rev. A. B. Cooper Senior (standing, left), Daddy (Dr. A. B. Cooper Jr., standing, right), Sergeant A. B. Cooper III of the U.S. Air Force, and baby A. B. Cooper IV pose for the photographer.

Before he left for work that day, I asked Daddy what he'd like for lunch. He said he thought we should use up the ground beef that he'd bought a few days ago, since we were leaving town tomorrow. He said, "Make some chili." Daddy always did the grocery shopping and basically planned our meals. So I prepared the chili, and when he came home, that's what we had for lunch. I think he ate a little more than he would normally because he knew we'd be gone and he didn't want to waste the food. After lunch, he sat out on the back doorstep with a warm foot bath to soothe his feet before returning to the office for his afternoon appointments.

I was sitting on my chaise lounge in my bedroom, sewing beads on one of the evening dresses I planned to take on the trip. The phone rang and it was Daddy's nurse telling me to come to the office as quickly as possible because Dr. Cooper had taken sick. I thought, Oh my goodness, all that chili made him sick—I've made Daddy ill.

Daddy and I had become proud grandparents ten times over by the time this photograph was taken. As you can see, boys ran in the family!

I was so nervous, I left immediately. I stopped by A. B. III's gas station and told him Daddy was sick and would he please stop whatever he was doing and drive me to the office. A. B. III told me he'd just received the call about Daddy; he closed up the station and drove me to the office. He dropped me off at the entrance and told me to go on up while he found a place to park.

When I reached the second floor, the hall was full of people. I made my way through, and Dr. Billings came to me and said, "Ann, he's gone."

Well, my first reaction was "Gone where?" Dr. Billings looked at my confused face and muttered, "Oh, I didn't do that right." And that's when he told me Daddy was dead. He'd been struck down by a massive heart attack.

Dr. Billings took me to his office to wait for A. B. III and Gwen to arrive. I think I must have fainted, because I remember waking up with his hand on my leg. They were getting ready to give me a shot of something in the thigh—a sedative, probably. But I wouldn't let them. Daddy always told me: "If something ever happens to me, you should refuse all kinds of sedation—any kind of pill or injection. You need to be aware of what's going on around you."

A. B. Gone.

They didn't want me to see Daddy in his current state, and I have to confess, I wanted only to remember him as the man who had kissed me good-bye that morning. The mortician was a family friend and neighbor, and she promised that when I saw Daddy next he would look the way he usually did. I trusted her to do that. But I told her I wanted her to do something else for me: "I want you to bring him to the house when you're done."

Most people thought I'd lost my mind from grief, but I knew what I was doing. When my own dear mama died, she stayed at home with us, in the living room, until the funeral service. And when I moved to Nashville, I remember one of our uncles dying and being laid out in Aunt Joyce's house. It stands out in my memory because I was maybe sixteen and was just starting to be allowed to have young men come to call. I remember thinking, Oh no! They can't come and find Uncle so-and-so stretched out in here—they'll never come back!

OVERLEAF: *A. B. III and Ann Marie* (LEFT). *Joyce and Gwen* (RIGHT). ⟶⟐

So I swore that wasn't ever going to happen in any house *I* might live in. Just goes to show you: never say never. Because all of a sudden, it made perfect sense to me that my husband and my children's father should be in the company of the people who loved him best, in the place he loved best. So we rearranged the living room furniture so that he and the visitors who came to see him—and us—would be comfortable, and for several days he was at home before we all went to First Congregational for his service. He was never alone.

The service was modest. I didn't want a big show. For one thing, I wasn't up to it and I don't think the children and their families were either. And you know how some funeral goers are: they come because they're curious and that's about it. I didn't want that. So we

---

&°— *Me, in the late fifties, sitting at a drop-leaf desk that has been in my family for generations. It came from Wessyngton Plantation, where one of my ancestors worked (and was the son of the owner), then went to Nashville, where it was handed down to Aunt Joyce's father, Granville. When he died, it came to Aunt Joyce, and, eventually, to me. I used to love to sit and write looooong letters on it. It has a place of honor in my den.*

---

invited family, of course, and good friends and patients that had been close to Daddy.

A few days before the funeral, the phone rang. Joyce answered it; her family had come the longest distance—all the way from California. I couldn't hear what she was saying, but she had this funny expression on her face.

"Who is it?" I whispered. It had been a long day. I felt as if I couldn't take any more condolences.

"A man who says his name is Daddy," Joyce whispered back.

Well, if that was a joke, it wasn't a very good one. Joyce continued to listen and her face cleared up.

"Oh. Ohhhhh. Yes, sir, I'll tell her." She hung up the phone and looked at me.

"That was Daddy *King.* He said to please tell you that he and Mrs. King would not be able to make the viewing today, but they will most certainly be at Daddy's services. He didn't want you to worry that they might not make it."

Another fifties' snapshot of Daddy and me, taken before we went out to some holiday party. I don't remember the exact year, but I do remember it was around Christmas. And look at Daddy—he's actually smiling!   —◦➤

I had completely forgotten that we called M. L.'s father Daddy, just as we did A. B. Well, that was good; it would be nice to have him and Alberta there. M. L.— or Martin Luther King Jr.—and Coretta would not be there. They'd already sent a beautiful telegram, telling us they were out of the country and had heard the news, probably from his parents. In those days, telegrams were horrendously expensive, and this one was one long page and must have cost a fortune. The Kings wrote how much Daddy meant to their family and to our community, and urged us to keep faith because faith will get you through:

May you gain consolation from the fact that you have a host of friends who are spiritually with you through these difficult and trying days . . . I know you will also gain additional consolation from the invincible surmise of the Christian faith, which affirms that death is not a blind alley that leads the human race into a state of nothingness, but an open door that leads men into life eternal

---

❦•— Gwen's first marriage ended in divorce. She had a happy second marriage and three children with Kenesaw Mannings. This photo was taken on their wedding day.

I DON'T REMEMBER MUCH of the service. All our family came. Many friends came from out of town, including Daddy's best and dearest friend, Dr. Hayley Bell, all the way from Detroit. They were as close as brothers. I do recall Hayley going up to A. B., looking at him for a long time, and patting him gently on the cheek. A brother's good-bye.

The church was full. They ran lovely obituaries in the *Atlanta Daily World,* our black paper, and the *Atlanta Journal-Constitution,* the mainstream paper. Daddy would have been proud.

You know the worst part of a loved one's passing isn't the funeral, it's afterward, when everyone goes back home to their established routines and you are left alone to deal with your loss. Your house seems so quiet, and mine reminded me of my loss every minute. Daddy wasn't a chatty man, but we spent time together each night, usually in the den, reading the evening papers and maybe watching a little television after dinner. The room was modest in size, but it seemed huge and empty with no Daddy in it anymore.

Me and A. B., with our grandchildren and Ann Marie, on the right. —⊶❧

I knew I would get back to being myself at some point, and I knew I would eventually have to figure out how to get on without Daddy. But right then, I didn't want to do any of that. I just wanted to keep to myself and be quiet. I thought my life was over, really.

It would take me a few years to realize that I was wrong.

CHAPTER ELEVEN

Getting Back Up Again

I WON'T LIE, AFTER we buried Daddy, it was hard to think about going on. We had been married for forty-five years, and you don't get over the loss of someone you've been with that long very easily. The process was going to be hard.

I spent a few months by myself, mulling things over and trying to clean out Daddy's effects. I really didn't want to do this. It was so difficult because every time I put something in a box or took something else out of the closet, it just made me realize anew the impact of his passing. I gave some of his things to our children and grandchildren, and to others, a bit at a time. I'd return to the task when I could emotionally cope again.

I had to realize that for the first time in my life, I would be on my own. I'd gone from living in the little country house in Bedford County to living in Nashville with Aunt Joyce, Uncle Jerry, and Irene to married life with Daddy. So I'd always had someone looking out for me, and the fact that I no longer did was a huge change. I did spent a few weeks being sad, but I knew some things needed taking care of. So I had to get myself up.

For one thing, there were bills to pay, and I had to find out how much and to whom. Luckily for me, Daddy kept impeccable financial records, so I could see what was what. He'd bought some up-to-date medical equipment that wasn't completely paid off, so I took care of that. One hundred dollars at a time, until it was all paid up. I went from never having to write a check to writing plenty of them!

We had always had a housekeeper. When the children were young, someone came every day to look after them while I was doing my volunteer work. Unlike most men at that time, Daddy was the one who did the grocery shopping. He liked thinking about what we were going to have for dinner. I think it relaxed him to roll down the aisles of the supermarket, checking the vegetables and inspecting the meat, until he got exactly what he wanted how he wanted it.

When he'd leave in the morning, he'd say, "I feel like steak for dinner tonight; how does that sound?" and I'd tell him to go ahead and get the meat. By the time he arrived at home we'd have the salad and the baked potatoes all done. It was a nice way to start the evening.

Since Daddy usually bought the groceries, I didn't spend much time fretting over what anything cost. Now, *I* was doing the marketing and had to consider cost. Gwen's son Eric came to stay with me for a few years after he got out of the army. It was nice to have someone in the house again, and Eric would drive me anywhere I wanted to go, including the grocery store. One day as Eric and I were standing in line with our cartload of purchases, I learned something new. I heard the cashier tell the lady ahead of us what her groceries came to and I saw the customer give the cashier several little pieces of paper. He tallied what was on them up and quoted her a different total—one that was much less.

"Eric, what is that she gave that man?" I whispered.

"Maybelle [that's his nickname for me], you've seen coupons before, haven't you?" He looked surprised.

"Where do you get them?" I whispered again. I'm sure I'd seen them from time to time, but since I didn't do the shopping, I didn't pay much attention.

"In your newspaper—you just cut them out and bring them to the store and they give you five, ten, sometimes even twenty cents off."

Well, wasn't that something? I wanted to get out of line, put everything back, go home, clip coupons, and start all over. Eric made the point that we'd be spending energy and gas doing that, and it probably wouldn't save us very much at the end. But I decided that from now on, I was clipping coupons.

After that, my biggest thrill was to come home with, say, a fresh half-gallon of milk. I would look at the almost-empty old one and say to Eric, "How much did you pay for that?" He would tell me, and I'd show him my receipt—I'd gotten my milk for seventeen cents less. Ha! Maybelle was definitely getting the hang of this coupon business. Even when people shop for me, even today, I tell them "check and see if we have a coupon for that." I don't mind spending money, but I hate wasting it. And if you don't use your coupons, you're leaving money on the table.

I find the nicest produce in stores that aren't so fancy—something else I learned in my newfound independence. I like to go down to Big Bear—it's kind of like a discount supermarket—because they have beautiful things like greens, celery, and tomatoes for way less than the big chain stores. And ham hocks? You can't even find those in some of these big stores. They're too uppity to carry them. How else are you going to make a good pot of greens or green beans without a decent ham hock?

So I like going down to Big Bear, but now I have to just about bribe my grandchildren to take me. "Granny, this is so deep in the hood, you don't need to be here and neither do I!" one told me. Oh yes, I do, I always say. I'll go a considerable distance for a good ham hock. I'm not going to be making anyone a second-rate meal. If I can do it for less money, so much the better.

I am cost-conscious when shopping for clothes, too. I've had dresses made for me and I've bought them straight off the rack. But some of my favorite dresses are sale dresses. I just *love* buying a dress that once went for some outrageous price for far less money when it goes on sale. I always told my girls: there's no shame in buying a $20 dress when its original price was many times that. Buying a quality item on sale is a better deal than buying a cheap dress at full price. Clothes cost much less now, though, than they did when I was a young wife and mother. It seems like everyone has a closet full of clothes. Oddly enough, they often say they feel like they don't have all that much that's nice to wear. I think that they must be shopping all the time, rather than waiting to shop the sales for good things, as we used to do.

Even today, I like a good sale dress or a good shoe on sale. I like to go out to Lenox Square and Phipps Plaza, in Atlanta's fancy Buckhead neighborhood, and look in all the nice stores. I've gotten some nice bargains there, too, let me tell you. I like a $200 high heel so much better when it's gone on sale for $80!

Before I broke my hip, high heels were the only shoes I ever wanted to wear. Here I chose white leather high-heeled boots to complete my cranberry-velvet birthday outfit. Just because I was turning one hundred two didn't mean I was going to dress like an old lady! —◦≫

CHAPTER TWELVE

Years of Promise

A S DADDY TOLD ME over the years so many times I can't count: *"Atlanta isn't Nashville."* By that he meant that I should not challenge white people—especially white men—when they try to put us down. I listened to him, mostly, but sometimes I couldn't help myself. I felt I was as good as the next person, I don't care what his color, and I always told that to my children: "Hold your head high—you are as good as anyone on this earth." I couldn't tell them one thing and act another way, but sometimes it got me in trouble.

Atlanta's public transportation system was segregated, of course, when Daddy and I moved to town in 1922. Like just about everywhere, we sat in the back and the white folks sat in the front. When the bus was crowded and seats were in short supply, we had to get up from the seats in the back. It was that way all over the South.

Some years before the buses and trolleys were desegregated, I was riding home from downtown on the trolley. Now back then, black people could enter at the front to pay the fare, but we had to exit from the rear. The city has built up and out now, but back then, we had to take the trolley to the last stop on Hunter. Then the conductor would turn it around and go back to town. Well, when he stopped this time, I was the last one on the trolley and, without thinking, I got off at the front and started walking toward home. The conductor, an older white man, was furious.

"You! Nigger! Come back here and go out the back like you're supposed do!"

Well, what kind of sense did that make? I wasn't going to walk back, get on the trolley again, and *then* get off at the back door. So I just kept walking. And he kept hollering all the terrible things that were going to happen to me if I didn't get back on that trolley and walk out the back.

"You better get back here, you black so-and-so!" he fumed.

"Really? Who's going to make me?" I was that angry! "You'd better leave on out of here and hope I don't tell my husband how you're talking to me!"

I don't think it scared him—but he left.

On another occasion a white man tried to put me out of my seat. It was after the streetcars and buses were desegregated, in 1959. I was on the bus riding home and sitting near the front. A white man sitting behind me was just furious that I had placed myself in front of him. He kept kicking the back of the seat and hissing "Get outta that seat, nigger."

He jostled me, but I wasn't going to let him or anybody else tell me what to do. I just clutched my purse and looked straight ahead and hoped I wasn't shaking for reasons other than his rude seat kicking.

He was making quite a ruckus, this man. The bus driver saw him but pretended otherwise, so he wouldn't have to get involved. That was typical behavior: if a white passenger acted up, the driver would "support" the bad behavior with his silence. They'd put a black passenger off the bus in a minute and radio for the police to be there waiting. I was getting thump-thump-thumped and trying to figure out what Daddy would say if he had to come down to jail to bail me out, because in half a minute, I was about to start doing some thumping of my own—with my handbag.

Then I saw a shape out the corner of my eye. A black man who had been quietly sitting toward the back had come up and was standing over me, holding onto the strap on the rail. He didn't say anything—just looked at me and gave a silent nod. I smiled back.

Thumper got the message. The kicks stopped. He just sulked and sucked his teeth until he got to his stop and stomped off. I can't tell you how protected I felt by the presence of my silent brown angel. He never told me his name, just tipped his hat and left the bus. But let me tell you, when people start to criticize and bash black men, I have to say: I have been lucky enough in my hundred-plus years to know hundreds, maybe thousands of good black men, and I thank God for every one of them.

So there were little personal rebellions like mine—and my angel's—going on all day, every day, when Atlanta was still segregated. For doctors and dentists and lawyers sometimes just staying in business was an act of rebellion. The white doctors didn't want us black folks in their waiting rooms, but they wanted our money. The big hospitals wouldn't treat black citizens, not even the public hospitals that welcomed the taxes we paid to keep them in business. When our medical people opened their own practices to serve our community, the white folks didn't like that very much, either—a no-win situation.

This was our dilemma locally, but the federal government wasn't always much better, including the Internal Revenue Service. The IRS used to harass black medical professionals terribly because they just assumed the doctors and dentists were taking cash payments and not reporting them. Even when the black men opened their books for inspection, the IRS didn't trust them. So they often sent investigators to each person's practice to sit in the waiting room and count the number of patients and nag the receptionist about how much was taken in and whether it was all going to be reported.

It was harassment, plain and simple, and it literally made some people sick. Many people developed high blood pressure or depression because the government was on their backs so much. And Lord help you if you had a sloppy bookkeeper! If you couldn't explain, to the last penny, every single charge and purchase, you were in for a terrible time. White professionals didn't have to endure that kind of treatment.

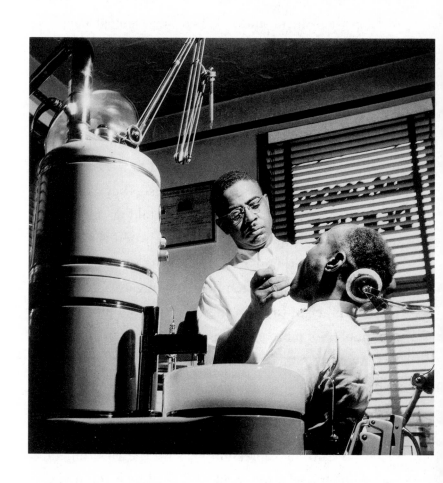

Thankfully, Daddy was just as compulsive about how his books were kept as he was about everything else. He spent many nights going over accounts and double-checking, to make sure the entries were right and the government was getting its money.

Atlanta likes to refer to itself as "the city too busy to hate." But back then, it was a city divided: black on one side and white on the other. This was the case even as some doctors, lawyers, businessmen, and clergy up and down Auburn Avenue exerted whatever pressure they could to remove those racial barriers. Historically, Auburn Avenue was the center of black business in Atlanta and was once referred to as "the richest Negro street in the world." Our local black men pointed out to the powers that be that places such as Montgomery, Alabama, where Martin Luther King and other ministers had successfully led a fifteen-month boycott of that city's public transportation system, were effecting changes for the better. The Montgomery boycott achieved gains for black people. For Montgomery's *big mules*—the city's white civic and social leaders—that act of social protest was expensive and embarrassing. Atlanta's white leaders hoped nothing like it would happen to them.

❦⚬— *Daddy at work.*

There was some give and take occurring around racial issues in the mid-twentieth century; some "two steps forward and one step back" kind of action. But in the winter of 1960, something big happened: the students at Atlanta University Center decided they'd been patient enough with the pace of racial progress. After several meetings called in black-owned restaurants such as Paschal's and Frazier's Café Society, near the AU Center, some students got together and published a long article called "An Appeal for Human Rights." The piece was published in Atlanta's black newspapers and riled plenty of people. Even folk in the white community who normally didn't read black publications saw the article and were upset. It was also published up North, in the *New York Times,* the following winter and that's when the roof fell in.

Everybody but the students who came up with the idea was upset. Here's this forward-thinking Southern city all of a sudden not looking so forward-thinking. Atlanta's white leaders were outraged that "their" black students had spoken up—and to a Yankee paper. The Old Black Guard—including A. B.—felt that the young ones were taking things too far too quickly. They feared that the consequences might undo all the progress their elders had painstakingly made. Oh, a huge fuss was made. Students from some of Atlanta's best black families were deeply involved, and there was no turning back. The young folk had gotten a taste of power and a glimpse of the world they were going to inherit, so they weren't too interested in going slow. They welcomed the change that was coming. The older Auburn Avenue men might not have been out demonstrating, but that didn't mean they weren't interested in equality. They may not have marched, but they hosted meetings, quietly paid bail bonds, and would treat injured protestors for free. They were another facet of the struggle that often wasn't seen or talked about, but was critical.

So with the older men pushing from one end and the young students of both genders squeezing from the other, some progress was made. The buses were desegregated in 1959. In 1960, demonstrations outside Rich's and several other downtown department stores resulted in a mass boycott by black folks who had gotten tired of paying their money to buy things there and not getting treated the same as white customers. During one demonstration, several AUC professors and Dr. King were all arrested and hauled off to jail.

All this went on during the presidential elections of 1960. Robert Kennedy got a lot of black votes in Atlanta for his brother John, because he personally called the judge who'd locked up M. L., Judge Oscar Mitchell, and asked him to release M. L. as a personal favor. Richard Nixon never picked up the phone. So you know who got our vote in that election.

The demonstrations continued, but now they were joined by white students from predominantly white schools like Emory and Georgia Tech, so you can imagine how upset the white community was getting. But the protests were working. By September of the following year, the merchants who upheld racist practices gave in. Now no matter what color you were, you could shop the downtown stores and sit down at the counter and have a Coke if you wanted to take a break.

I don't even drink soda, but I had to sit down and have one after that. At Rich's, of course. And after that, it was always nice to stop and have lunch in the tea room if I needed a break while I was shopping.

The schools were desegregated that same year as well, at least on paper. The University of Georgia took in two black students, Charlayne Hunter and Hamilton Holmes, in 1961. That was supposed to trigger the official and complete desegregation of the public school system from elementary through high school. But the white people fought and fought to keep "their" schools white and managed to take only a few of us at a time. It wasn't until almost ten years later that the schools really and truly integrated to any significant degree.

Since his return to Atlanta in 1960 from Alabama, M. L. had been working alongside the students and the older civic leaders to desegregate Georgia. Our community just about burst with pride when it was announced that, for his earlier work in Montgomery and for his general philosophy of nonviolent resistance, Daddy King and Alberta's baby boy was going to be given the Nobel Peace Prize.

The prize included a gold medal and more than fifty thousand dollars. M. L. promptly announced that he was going to use the money to further the civil rights movement. But on the personal side, I wonder if Coretta was so thrilled about that. He had been away from home a lot, and she had had the task of raising four children on a young minister's skimpy salary. That money could have made life a lot easier for them, but M. L. felt that it belonged to the community. That brought him even more respect—but I suspect it exasperated Coretta not to even have been consulted. It would have me.

When M. L. and Coretta returned from the medal ceremony in Stockholm that December, there was a huge party in his honor at one of the big, newly de-segregated downtown hotels, and we all went down to celebrate. The affair was elegant, but a lot of us came down with food poisoning. We were sick as dogs by the wee hours of the morning. Some people believed we'd been deliberately poisoned, but Daddy concluded otherwise. "No way you can feed five hundred people hot food at once—some of that stuff has probably been waiting for hours," he said. Maybe he was right. Even with the stomach troubles, the evening had been lovely.

If I could do it over again I would—but I'd have only the salad.

OVERLEAF, LEFT: *Ambassador Andrew Young is a good family friend and a particular favorite of mine. He began this tradition of giving me a gold charm for every one of my birthdays since I turned ninety-nine. Here, he's presenting me with the latest, a gold filigree cross with "102" in the middle of it. Now the "101" charm I had been wearing as a pendant will come off and join the others on my bracelet, and the "102" will hang around my neck.*

OVERLEAF, RIGHT: *Ambassador and Mrs. Andrew Young, the Birthday Girl, and Mr. Sarkis Agasarkisian, who designs and makes the gold charms that Andy gives me each year.* ⟶◦❧

CHAPTER THIRTEEN

Years of Pain

THE CIVIL RIGHTS MOVEMENT had achieved a better quality of life in Atlanta; the downtown stores, buses, and some businesses had been desegregated. There was still work to be done, though. And exercising our right to vote was a way to accomplish the goals yet to be met. I had voted since at least right after the Second World War, but not everyone felt comfortable doing so—especially people in the state and around the South outside Atlanta. But organizations such as the Southern Christian Leadership Conference (SCLC), founded by Martin Luther King Jr.,

Ralph David Abernathy, Fred Shuttlesworth, Joseph Lowery, and other ministers, were committed and making strides. These were heady times.

And violent ones. I was so glad that Joyce was out in California, away from the violence of Freedom Summer 1964, and that Tootie (Ann Marie) and Gwen were not in the middle of the turbulence going on in some other parts of the country. A. B. III, my son, on the other hand, was like Information Central. The gas station he owned was right across the street from Paschal's restaurant and everyone supported it and used it to exchange information and sort out rumors. I watched the evening news every night before dinner, but you can bet I also always called A. B. to ask, "What did you hear today?"

Atlanta became known for the Atlanta University Center, the Coca-Cola Company, which was based there, and for our comparatively forward-thinking attitudes about race largely of course because of the civil rights movement and Martin Luther King Jr. After he won his Nobel Peace Prize, M. L. continued his work, but he had come to see that relief from poverty was as much a civil right as being free to shop and ride public transportation. He expanded his work to include efforts to achieve economic justice and began taking the fight for equality beyond the South, to the North. As a consequence, he was met with

stiff opposition in many communities. Whenever some
uppity Northerner tells us about how bad the South is,
I say one thing to him: "Cairo." I refer to those "enlight-
ened" Yankees in that Chicago suburb who were about
as nasty and violent as the rednecks Martin ran into on
marches in the South. I think he was shocked at their behavior. Los Angeles also had its share of racial problems
and had burned up in the Watts riots of 1965. And Detroit, where our friends the Hayley Bells lived, erupted in
racial violence in 1966. All told, more than one hundred
big cities, mostly in the North, went up in flames. There
was a lot of restlessness and anger there.

Then came the saddest day: when we got news that
Martin had been killed in Memphis. I'll never forget
it—April 4, 1968.

Things had been getting so ugly. The Kings' home
had been bombed, and there wasn't a week that went
by that he didn't get some kind of terrible death threat.
We perhaps shouldn't have been shocked, but we were.
Our first thoughts were for Martin's family—Coretta,
her children, and his parents. But *murder*! To lose such a
man in the prime of his life, when his children were just
babies, really. That was heartbreaking. I was devastated
when Daddy died, but at least I had the consolation that
his children had had him until they reached adulthood.

Yoki—Yolanda—was the Kings' oldest and she was only twelve. The baby, Bernice, wasn't even in school yet.

Our second thought was concern for Atlanta. We knew people would be angry and wondered if the anger would boil over into rioting. So everything was very tense. But Atlanta held. It held for its hometown son, I think. On the day of M. L.'s funeral services, people streamed into the streets to say a last good-bye. If you've seen films of the church service or were old enough and in Atlanta to witness it yourself, you know people were packed in the place like sardines, and several folk passed out from the emotion and the heat.

Coretta was like a queen: serene and dignified. She did for the nation what Mrs. Kennedy had done for us five years earlier—she led us by graceful example. There was no wailing or thrashing. The whole church was stoic and dignified in its grief.

And outdoors people waited for the service to be over and then they fell in behind M. L.'s casket, which was mounted on a wooden wagon pulled by mules, the symbol of M. L.'s connection to the poor people of the nation and the world. Thousands of people lined the street to watch M. L.'s casket pass from his family's church to his alma mater, Morehouse College, where another public service was held so more people could participate.

I tell you, remembering that day still brings tears to my eyes. I think in part because M. L.'s death followed Daddy's so closely. Just a few months later, Bobby Kennedy suffered the same fate as M. L. while campaigning for president out in California. It made you wonder: Why was America steadily killing off the people who were most successful in bringing us the greatest hope? But as M. L. had written in his telegram after Daddy died, faith will get you through. So I had to hold on and have faith that these terrible, painful years would pass and that there were better times on the other side.

But for a few years, it certainly didn't feel that way.

The Personal and the Political

The AU Center campus remained at the center of the social and political changes that continued. One new trend that made me smile but probably had Daddy rolling over in his grave had to do with grooming. Otherwise neatly dressed students were now growing Afros, which was funny, because the few African students who'd been over to our house tended to wear close-cut hair. The black American students' new hairdos were big and so nappy they used a pick to achieve the style. I used the same kind of fork to cut angel food cake for the ladies when I hosted a tea that some of the young folk used to comb their hair. Even the students who had hair that *didn't* nap up too well did their best to make it curl and coil tightly. Personally, I didn't see the point. Your hair is your hair—why make it crazy by forcing it to do something it doesn't want to? Although come to think of it, we do that when we straighten our hair or dye the gray out of it. I guess it's just human to want to change your appearance from time to time. Young people, including my daughter Ann Marie, our Tootie, have to do something to be different from us old folks, and that's one of the things that came in with the 1960s. I didn't even argue with Tootie. All my children are just like me anyway: stubborn.

I know there were arguments being had at dinner tables all over black America when these students came home with their nappy hair all out to there and their parents wanting to know why they couldn't look more "respectable."

The other thing happening that was more worrisome was students and other young people questioning whether M. L.'s passive resistance approach to protest was going to work much longer. They were getting more militant, and they didn't want to be called *Negro* anymore. They were black—and the conversation was about black this and black that. I'm using the term *black* throughout this book. But I've lived long enough to see our collective attitudes change along with our preference for what we're called that I just decided to use one term consistently. When I was coming up, polite black people called themselves "colored." Then, around the Second World War, we started calling ourselves Negro. For a while, we were Afro-American, but not everybody everywhere embraced that term. After that, the young people wanted us to be called black. And let me tell you, that took some getting used to for many of us, because back in the old days, if you called somebody black, they'd hit you. We were black until sometime after Jesse Jackson first ran for president. He started referring to himself and us as African Americans. But that wasn't me. I had had just about enough of the Name Game by that time. For one thing, "African American" is just a mouthful to have to say. And for another, what's wrong with plain old black? So it's fine that Jesse and anybody else who wants to can be African American, but call me *black,* please.

The year Daddy died, Julian Bond, a young black political activist and the son of close friends, finally got his

seat in the Georgia State House of Representatives. He'd been elected a few years earlier but had been blocked from taking his seat by other representative who didn't like his opposition to the Vietnam War. Bond turned out to be right. But he had to win his seat two more times before he began to serve. So he was now, finally, going to represent our district in the Georgia Legislature, and we were sure there was going to be some fireworks as a result. Though Julian had a boyish face, he thought and spoke quickly on his feet. Some of those good ol' boys weren't going to know what hit them.

❧— *Ready for a trip to town! Ann Marie, Gwen, and Joyce. Note that they are all wearing dresses that were the height of daytime fashion at the time: Ann Marie and Gwen had sleeveless sheaths, and Joyce had a crisp shirtwaist. And everyone had white cotton gloves—the uniform of middle-class black women everywhere at that time.*

OVERLEAF, LEFT: *Ann Marie's wedding. Gwen and Joyce flank their baby sister on her big day before she goes off to First Congregational Church to be wed.*

OVERLEAF, RIGHT: *A. B. Cooper III, handsome in uniform.*

So change abounded—even personal changes for me. I bought my first pantsuit—something I never would have done when my husband was alive. He thought women belonged in dresses, just not too-short ones. His rule applied especially to me. My girls were full-grown and didn't wear real short dresses either, but some that they wore were above the knee. They had inherited their mother's legs, so I thought they looked right cute. And one of the world's best inventions started showing up in the stores: panty hose. No more girdles and garter belts. Women today take panty hose for granted. So many fashions, though, come back around. I chuckle now, for example, when I see how some of our young women are wearing stockings again—it's a novelty for them. They're also going back to girdles, but now call them body shapers. They're made of all that new material. My granddaughters and great-grands love them. As far as I'm concerned, they can have them. Granny will keep her panty hose and her knee-highs and stay away from girdles no matter what you call them, thank you very much.

CHAPTER FOURTEEN

So Rich in Blessings

PEOPLE OFTEN SAY THE first part of your life goes by slowly and the second part just zips on by, and I've certainly found that to be true. Looking back, it feels as if it was just yesterday that I was burning my initials onto my arm with my sisters. The only initials I have anywhere these days are on my stationery, my sterling flatware, and my monogrammed jewelry. Now, here I am with great-grandchildren who may be doing some of the same silly things that young people always have. Mercifully, their parents and grandparents don't worry me with them—such as trips they've taken to the emergency room due to rough-housing. (I know that prob-ably happens, because boys run in our family, and you know how boys are.)

I am happy to say that all my children grew up to marry and have wonderful families of their own. My oldest daughter, Gwen, went to medical school and practiced as an internist. She had three boys: Kenny, Eric, and Albert.

Joyce became a teacher, married a surgeon, and moved to California, where she, too, had three boys: Joseph (we call him Randy), Larry, and Christopher.

A. B. III owned that Gulf service station in the heart of Atlanta's black community. He married twice and had five children: A. B. IV (we call him B. B.), Michael, Sheila, Anthony (Tony), and Jeffrey.

And Ann Marie, our baby, became a French profes-sor at Florida A&M University and had four children: Gerald, Ernest, Theresa, and Gwen Joyce.

Between them, they raised lawyers, judges, artists, actors, professors, and journalists—even a licensed massage therapist. (That's Gwen Joyce, and you can bet Granny enjoys having a massage when she comes to visit.)

So I am immensely proud of my children and my grandchildren, and their children and grandchildren, too. I have listed everyone in the back of this book so you can see the little dynasty Daddy and I began. Gwen and Tootie both died of cancer, and after years of increasing frailty, A. B. III died of Parkinson's disease.

I have to think that if my three children had been sick these days, they might have made it. Even in twenty years there has been so much progress in how cancer is detected and how it is fought. Their chances would have been so much better. Losing a child is the worst thing that can happen to a parent, and it has happened to me three times. Sometimes I have been so sad over that, it feels like I cannot get up in the morning. But M. L. was right: faith will get you through.

And anyway, I had grandchildren I needed to help raise. That's what kept me going.

I really enjoyed feeding my tribe, so that kept us busy. We'd plan our meals, go to the grocery store, and then I'd cook a big roast—often my favorite, lamb—and a big casserole of sweet potatoes or macaroni, and make a big pot of turnip greens. And the grands would come over for dinner. (And let me tell you, those boys could *eat!*)

Some of our happiest times were around the dining room table. When all the children were alive, no matter where they were living, they would return to Atlanta

at Christmas. I always had a big Christmas dinner the Sunday following Christmas, and as the children had children, it got bigger every year.

They would drive in or fly in, all the little ones lugging their favorite Christmas gifts (and waiting to see what Daddy and I had given them) and on that Sunday, we would all go to church, then come home for Granny's big dinner. I would have someone help me pull out the dining room table to its fullest, using every leaf. We would put on the extra-long table linens I'd had made for that purpose. Then we'd set up three or four card tables in the living room for the youngsters.

All the tables—the big one and the little ones—would be decorated with vases of red and white flowers and evergreens. Sometimes we'd spread extra Christmas ornaments on the tabletops. The table would be set with my best silver and china, and after saying grace (which I know some of the grands thought was too long), we would just feast and laugh all afternoon.

Those were happy, happy times.

Let me tell you, dancing will keep you young! Here I am with my grandson Ernest, dancing at his sister Theresa's wedding in Tallahassee in 1983.

I still like to set a good table and invite people in. Until I was about one hundred five, I did a lot of the cooking myself.

Now, don't feel sorry for me rattling around in this house by myself, because I haven't. I was lucky enough to have a couple of Gwen's children come and stay with me for a few years, and Tootie's children visited often. And I have people who weren't blood relatives who became like family to me: Bettye, Sally, and James.

Bettye Sue Hudson was a young college girl from the little town of Dyersburg, Tennessee, near Nashville. She and I became friends by a lovely twist of fate. Bettye had graduated from the University of Tennessee and thought she wanted to go live in the big city, so she was offered a job in Atlanta and came down here. They were supposed to put her in the YWCA, but when she got there, they'd messed up her placement, so they offered to put her in a family home.

Well, lucky for me, the first one didn't suit her, and the person trying to find her a place said, "I know someone who lost her husband last year, and she might like

---

In May 1980, I received an important Community Service Award from WXIA-TV in Atlanta. I was seventy-eight years old. —◦❧

some company. Let me see if she might consider having you stay with her."

And that's what happened. Despite our age difference—I was probably the age of Bettye's mother—we got along like two old friends. She would go off to work every morning, and when she returned, we'd sit down and have dinner together. Some weekends, we'd leave in the morning and go out and shop all day, just stopping for lunch.

Bettye was what I called "unformed." She showed up on my doorstep, this smart, polite, shy little country girl. I think I saw in her some of me, the me that first came to Atlanta in 1922. I thought if I could pass along some of what I'd had to learn on my own, it might help Bettye, if she was interested.

She was, and so we became thick as thieves. I taught her how to entertain, how to stretch a meal when unexpected company came, and how to make sure her guests were comfortable and well cared for. But maybe most important, I got her to understand that she should show herself off to her best advantage.

Bettye and I looked like Mutt and Jeff: here I was, middle-aged (okay, more, but I still had a young-looking face) and barely five feet, and Bettye was five feet eight. That's still considered tall these days, but now tall is in fashion. Back then, it wasn't. So Bettye would always wear flat shoes, even with dressy clothes. She told me, "I was the third-tallest girl in my high school, and it wasn't any fun." I can imagine she got tired of hearing "Hey, how's the air up there?" Which wasn't funny then and still isn't, if you ask me.

One day when we were shoe shopping, I watched as Bettye tried on boxes of flat shoes. I couldn't stand it anymore. "Look here," I said, pulling her over to the store's full-length mirror. "Look at you—really *look*." Bettye was looking at me like I was crazy. "Let me tell you what I see," I told her. "I see a girl with a very nice figure—tall, slender, with beautiful legs and nice feet and ankles and a little waist." I could see Bettye was looking to see what I saw.

"Bring us some heels in her size," I told the shoe man, and he hustled away. He came back with boxes of them, most of which looked quite nice on Bettye. So I told him we'd take two pairs. "From now on," I told her, "you put on those high heels and hold your head high. Always show off your best assets instead of hiding them!"

And that's exactly what Bettye did.

She lived with me for five years, total. Three years at first, then she thought she wanted to live up north, in

Connecticut. I was sad to see her go, but I figured she'd be coming back sometime soon, and two years later she did. She came back to stay with me and in a flash we were right back in our old habits—shopping, dinner together, and so on.

A couple years after that, Bettye had the opportunity to buy a house not far from me, and I told her, "Do it!" I believe in women owning property. For many years, before she retired and moved back to Tennessee, Bettye and I were around-the-corner neighbors. She still comes to visit a couple times a year, and I am always thrilled to see her.

Alberta Tucker also lived with me for a few years. Like Bettye, she went on to establish her own life, independent of mine. But she still lives in Atlanta, and we remain friends. Alberta will come and visit me every two weeks or so, and she will do my hair. If something big comes up, Alberta will come and make sure I look presentable.

I've known Sally Warner for a number of years. Her husband Clint's parents were friends of ours. I held Clint on my lap when he was a baby. He and my oldest, Gwen, were born the same year: 1924. Sally would run my New York friend Charlie Henderson from the airport to my house and back when she came to visit. After a while, we started calling each other between Charlie's visits. When my children were planning my hundredth birthday party, I needed someone nearby to check the details. Ann Marie lived in Tallahassee and Joyce in California. Ann Marie suggested I call Sally and ask her to help with the guest list. Sally said, "Sure." And that was that. We have been bosom buddies ever since. I tease Sally and tell friends she is part social secretary, part camp counselor, part publicist, part driver, and part bodyguard. When she doesn't want you to do something, it's going to be a real fight to get around her! I sometimes tease her and call her the White Lady, which she thinks is pretty funny. So if someone calls and wants me to attend something and she thinks it will wear me out too much, she'll just say, "Mrs. Cooper, don't you think you should give this some extra thought? You just got over a bad cold and here you are wanting to be in a room with all those people and their germs. You aren't going. No indeed!"

So I tell them "My white lady says no!" And we just laugh. It has gotten to be a joke among our closest friends. Sally is white, but not to me. To me, she is just my dear Sally.

And then there is James Davis. Sally calls James "Mrs. Cooper's boyfriend." Of course, I'm old enough to be James's grandmother, but he takes marvelous care of me. James is a cook, and we used to always run into him at various events. If it was a great party or gathering, James's catering company had prepared the food. Clint and Sally gave me a surprise birthday party when I turned one hundred and one. James came and gave me one of the greatest birthday gifts I've ever received: he decided he was going to take a major role in looking after me. He just said, "Mrs. Cooper, you need some help, and I'm it." And James just shows up whenever I need him to take me places, do little things around the house, and cook the most marvelous meals!

It was James and Sally who took on the task of finding good people to come stay with me when I decided I didn't need to stay by myself anymore. (Note it was *me* who was doing the deciding—no one made me do this.) First came Edwina Chester, a wonderful lady who was with me for a year and a half. But I'm a lot to keep up with, and I think I wore poor Edwina out, so she had to retire. Since then, Katrinka Davis and Shirley Allen have come into my life, courtesy of James and Sally.

James, Sally, and me in 2002 at a Christmas luncheon at Scholar's Restaurant, on the campus of Morris Brown College. —◦»

Katrinka and Shirley come to stay with me on alternate weeks, so they can rest up in between, and I can stay in my own house, where my family and friends come to check on me. I can't tell you how much it means to be in my own home, on my own terms. I know how blessed I am.

CHAPTER FIFTEEN

Try and Catch Up with Me!

I THINK IT WAS Julia Child who said, "You have to keep going—if you don't, you die." If it wasn't her, whoever said it was right: keeping moving keeps you going.

Until I was about one hundred something, I went to exercise class several times a week. It was a little aerobics class, and I really enjoyed it. It was a lot like dancing, which I did regularly until I was about one hundred four. Up until then, if you took me to a party, you didn't have to worry about sending people over to keep me company. I spent all my time out on the dance floor! My great-grandchildren would teach me the latest dances, and I loved doing them. I learned the Electric Slide and used to love to teach the old folks (most of whom were significantly younger than me) how to do that dance. At my one hundred fourth birthday party, there I was, leading the line!

Let me tell you, it was a good thing I stayed in shape, too: it gave me enough energy to try to catch a thief!

Here's how it happened: my good friend Marie Saxon and I had just come from working at church on a Friday afternoon and decided to go to the pharmacy on the way home and get that errand out of the way. Well, we were in the elevator of the Medical Building on MLK Jr. Drive (that's what they call Hunter Street now), when a young man got in. He asked us how we were doing, and Marie and I asked him how he was doing. Then, when the door opened, that man grabbed Marie's purse and ran off!

One hundred four and still cutting a rug! I loved doing the electric slide—you don't need a partner or anything, just a group of people who love to dance. I knew all the moves, so I would often teach people the sequences. And they'd have to look sharp to keep up with me. —◦➤

My good friend Marie Saxon came to help me celebrate my one hundred second birthday. We had become briefly famous when I was one hundred and Marie was eighty-five, when we chased down a purse snatcher on the streets of Atlanta. We had just come from church and were filling a prescription at the drugstore when this man snatched Marie's purse and we ran after him. A reporter came out to do a story on these two little old ladies who were trying to catch this robber. As Marie said at the time, "I don't know what we would have done if we'd caught him—look at us!" Neither of us weighed a hundred pounds after a big meal, and both of us were under five feet tall. We laughed about our vigilante adventure. (They never caught the man—but I hope he read the papers and was thoroughly ashamed of himself.) —•➤

Before we knew what we were doing, Marie and I were running after him, with Marie screaming "Give me back my pocketbook!" as loud as she could.

I know, we were crazy, right? Here both of us are, not even five feet tall. Marie was eighty-five and I had just turned one hundred. Together we probably weighed less than our robber—who was well over two hundred pounds. As I was chasing him with Marie, I suddenly thought: What if we catch him? We can't hold him! We need the police!

So I hollered for Marie to stop and I went to call 911. They never did get her things back. We had to cancel all her credit cards, change her locks, and disable her cell phone. It's a shame this happens in our community. You want to feel safe among your own people, after all, but it's the times, I guess. I often wonder if that man ever fessed up and told anyone that he'd snatched a purse and was chased down by two little old ladies. I wonder if he ever regretted it, after reading the write-up about Marie and me running after him.

My grandchildren snicker to this day when I say, "Don't make me chase you down, now . . ."

Turning one hundred is a big milestone, and my family had me turn one hundred in style. They came from all around the globe to help me celebrate. The party was in the Wyndham Atlanta Hotel, and when I say everybody came, I mean everybody and then some! It was great, great fun.

People came and stayed the week. My living room was filled with beautiful flowers. Champagne corks popped every day. There were lovely phone calls and messages from friends and relatives from around the country. I think we took enough pictures to keep Kodak and the digital camera people in business for a few years! (Such a change from when Daddy and I gave parties. Most of our photos came from a professional we hired to record the evening. And of course they were black and white. Now you can see the results instantly with those digital cameras. And when people take pictures of me and they come out bad, I make them erase them and do it over again!)

Also when I was one hundred, I had the honor of leading the litany at our church, First Congregational,

---

OVERLEAF: *The clan gathers to celebrate my one hundredth birthday: Coopers, Hoopers, Bobos, and Mannings and their spouses and children and grandchildren. People came from around the world to help me celebrate. We had a glorious time. The grandchildren got tired way before I did!* —◦❧

which is even older than I am. I was quite excited to be asked to do that.

My bridge club, the Jovial Coterie, still comes to my house sometimes for a few hands of bridge. And the Literary Club usually comes once a year so I can keep up with them. I go to a Links activity every now and then, which is always fun. Friends continue to stop by and visit, and that's always enjoyable. And of course I delight in seeing not only my grandchildren, but my great-grandchildren, some of whom are young adults themselves now and off at college.

And let me tell you: just because you are old doesn't mean you lose interest in everything. I keep up with the news—I am a big CNN fan—and try to learn at least one new thing every day. I also love *The Price is Right* and *Oprah*. I still love my high heels. I can't walk very far in them, but these days I don't need to: I have a walker for short distances and a wheelchair for long walks, and your heels can be as high as you want if you're in a wheelchair.

My one hundred second birthday.

I still insist on dressing well—I like looking sharp!

And I love having my nails done and wearing my favorite red lipstick. I tell you, even when you don't feel so good, if you get yourself up to look good, you'll feel better.

I don't know why, but that always works for me.

CHAPTER SIXTEEN

Never Thought I'd See the Day!

WELL, I'VE GOT YOU just about all caught up on my life, up to the point that everybody has come to know about, the part where Mrs. Cooper Goes to Vote. Now I can tell you how that came about.

I try not to get down in the dumps, but sometimes it happens. When you are my age, many, if not most, of your dear friends are gone. I have buried not only the love of my life, but three of my four darling children, one grandchild, and three great-grandchildren. The

past few years have brought some health problems—it would be unusual if I didn't have any, given my age—and I will tell you, between the celebrations and the keeping busy, sometimes I get a little down.

I was having one of those days last year when Sally and James decided they knew what I needed: some media attention!

Sally had a friend, Beverlyn Gordon, and I guess she told Beverlyn that this little one-hundred-six-year-old lady was going to vote in a week or so and that maybe that might be a nice human interest story for them. Beverlyn called her friend Audrey Hines, who is a producer at CNN.

Audrey called one of the news anchors there, Don Lemon, and told him about me, and before I knew it, he was at my doorstep wanting to know more. He asked if he could come and watch while I voted, and I told him I didn't see why not.

Well, I don't know who told everybody else (certainly not Don—he wanted that story all for himself!), but by the time we got to the Fulton County government

---

✥ *—Me and the late Margaret Washington Clifford, the granddaughter of Booker T. Washington.*

building, where they were doing the early voting, it seemed like all the Atlanta media was there. And they all had cameras and tape recorders.

My friend Shirley Franklin, the mayor of Atlanta, met me at the entrance, and Don wheeled me in. Were we surprised when we saw all those people there, waiting to watch me vote! I couldn't believe it!

So I got up out of my wheelchair, walked up to the computer screen that had all the candidates on it, and touched the screen to vote for Barack Obama. I tell you, I never thought I'd live to see the day when a black man would be a serious candidate for the office of President of the United States. A lot of history had happened to allow this moment to occur. A lot of people—black *and* white—had made sacrifices, even lost their lives, so we could be at this moment. I don't know how I knew, but I knew in a few months we would have President Obama.

Sally, James, and I went home and had a nice dinner. We saw me on the news—I must say, I looked pretty good for a little old lady!—and then I went on off to bed.

Who knew what I had created? Between election night and the inauguration, the phone rang and rang with re-

Me and former president Jimmy Carter and his wife, Rosalynn.

The Trumpet Awards, January 7, 2002

Me and Christine King Farris, Martin Luther King Jr.'s sister.

Me and Lerone Bennett Jr., executive editor emeritus of Ebony.

Me and Sidney Poitier. There's Marla Gibbs in the background.

Me and Nancy Wilson.

quests for interviews. Some were from people right here in town. Some were on the telephone. And a lot were from television crews from around the country and the world. It got harder and harder to get out of my driveway. Seems like there was always a camera crew blocking it.

And after the president-elect called my name during his victory speech, things got even crazier! Seems like every single day there was someone who wanted an interview, and none of them were short. I started to feel a little sympathy for people like Lena Horne, who must have gone through this all the time at the height of her fame, back in the '40s and '50s. Or that Beyoncé girl today.

But I have to confess, I loved it. I loved the *reason* for the attention as much as the attention. I am thrilled beyond words that the Obama family is in the White House, and that the world sees this young black family, with two smart, pretty children and highly accomplished parents as an example of what black is and can be. Lord knows, we've had enough bad examples. I am quite happy to have this excellent one.

I kind of felt like I'd done my job: I had helped to elect the first black president. So I didn't need to go to Washington to see this happen. I was not one of those people braving the cold to stand out on the Mall or in front of the Capitol to watch Barack Hussein Obama become the forty-fourth president of the United States. I watched from the comfort of my favorite chair, in my cozy den, surrounded by friends and family—and some of my new friends from the media. Afterward, we had a nice lunch to celebrate the occasion and after watching the new president and his wife have their first dance— so romantic!—I had a little sherry and went on up to pack. I'd actually developed a little cold after my one hundred-seventh birthday party the week before, and Sally, James, and Katrinka wanted to take me to the hospital on inauguration morning. But I wasn't about to leave my home without seeing the new president sworn in and take that first dance with his wife. So I refused to budge. But after the swearing-in, the luncheon, and the balls, I let them take me on over to the hospital. (It was a good thing; the cold had turned into pneumonia, so I had to stay for a little while.)

I felt like it was okay to go to the hospital now; I had done what I'd had to do, and I truly believed the country was going to be in good hands going forward. Even while I was watching the new president speak to the nation, the same thought kept running through my head: *I never thought I'd live to see the day.*

Who would have thought this little colored girl,

born in the countryside outside Nashville less than fifty years after the Civil War, would live to see the day a black man would lead the free world? Who would have thought that our country would have gotten to the point where so many people—people of all colors—were comfortable enough with the idea of equality that they elected him?

I couldn't have imagined it back then. But if living this long teaches you anything, it teaches you to prepare to be surprised every single day. And to keep an open mind to change, because a lot of those surprises could turn out to be good ones.

ACKNOWLEDGMENTS

A THOUSAND THANKS to my companions and help-mates: Bettye, Alberta, Edwina, Katrinka, Shirley, Phillipa, Sally, and James: where would I have been without you? Also to my extended family, of whom I am very proud. And to my many friends in the organizations I have belonged to over the years, especially at First Congregational Church of Atlanta. I love you all.

—Ann Nixon Cooper

My deepest gratitude goes to:
Malaika Adero and Todd Hunter, the team at Atria Books that guided Mrs. Cooper's story from idea to reality. Faith Hampton Childs, agent extraordinaire; Ellen Weiss, Philip Bruce, and my colleagues at NPR West.

The Bobo, Cooper, Hooper, and Mannings families for sharing stories about Mrs. Cooper, especially: Joyce Cooper Bobo and Christopher Bobo, Eric Mannings, Gwen Hooper, and A. B. Cooper IV.

Ashley Bobo for her research assistance. Rev. and Mrs. Norman Rates. Phillipa Brisbane. John F. Baker Jr. for his superb history of his ancestors: *The Washingtons of Wessyngton Plantation,* and his generosity in sharing that knowledge.

Dr. Clarissa Myrick-Harris, vice president, One World Archives, for her invaluable knowledge of Atlanta's civil rights history; Herman "Skip" Mason for his books *Black Atlanta in the Roaring Twenties* and *Politics, Civil Rights and Law in Black Atlanta, 1870–1970;* Gloria Wade-Gayles and the Spelman SIS Oral History Project. The Hon. Andrew Young. Bettye Sue Hudson. James Davis, Shirley Allen; Katrinka Davis; and most especially Sally E. J. Warner, who cheerfully and tirelessly tried to find answers to every question I tossed at her.

If there are any errors, they are mine and no one else's.

—*Karen Grigsby Bates*

THE COOPER CLAN
Descendants of Ann Louise Nixon Cooper and Albert Berry Cooper Jr.

First Generation

Ann Louise Nixon Cooper,
*Albert Berry Cooper Jr.

Second Generation

*Gwendolyn Yvonne Cooper
Joyce Nixon Cooper
*Albert Berry Cooper III
*Ann Marie Cooper

*deceased

Third & Fourth Generations

Gwen's children:
Kenesaw Mannings Jr.
Eric Mannings
Eric Patrick, Wesley, Alexandra Gwendolyn
Albert Mannings

Joyce's children:
Joseph Bobo
Alexis
Lawrence Bobo
Christopher Bobo
Ashley, Amanda

A. B. III's children:
A. B. Cooper IV ("B. B.")
*Brea, Ariel, *Kwanza*
Michael Cooper
**Christopher, *Mickey, Maya*
Anthony Cooper
T. J., Dalton
Jeffrey Cooper
Ainsley, Malcus, and Safiya
*Sheila Cooper

*deceased

Ann Marie's children:

Gerald Hooper

Ernest Hooper

Matthew, Ethan, Madelyn

Theresa Hooper

Rachel

Gwendolyn Joyce Hooper